Confidence & Self-Love

WORKBOOK FOR WOMEN

Real Ways to Love Yourself, Increase Your Self-Worth and and Be Confident in Who You Are

Roberta Sanders

TABLE OF CONTENTS

INTRODUCTION

Hello beautiful woman!

I am really happy you are reading this, because it probably means that some part of you, however big or small, is ready to stop the war you are waging with yourself. I created this workbook in order for you to start your own exploration. Take your time thinking about each question and be honest with your answers.

This workbook belongs to you, and only you. Write freely, write securely and most importantly be yourself ! You will find many tools and insights to build the best version of yourself so use the writing prompts in whichever way works and feels best for you.

You are the most important person in your life and the relationship you have with yourself is the most defining factor in shaping the kind of life you live.

The less you love yourself, understand yourself, and listen to yourself, the more confused, angry, and frustrating your reality will be. But when you start and continue to love yourself more, the more everything you see, everything you do, and everyone you interact with, starts to become a little bit better in every way possible.

Self-love isn't easy. As they say: you are your own biggest critic.

Our unconscious is programmed to have bouts of self-loathing, and for many of us, these phases of self-hatred can last our entire lives. It's when we spend more time hating ourselves than we do loving ourselves that we adopt a more negative disposition to the world. So, begin to love yourself first. It might not be the easiest thing in the world to do, but it's definitely the most important.

There are many women out there who want to have a companion in life, not because they really want a partner or because of society, but only because they want people to be by their side whenever they feel low in life or whenever life is just too overwhelming for them. It is perfectly fine to feel overwhelmed sometimes. If you have a partner (they can be your love partner or a friend or a family member) to talk to, then you are the lucky one. Even if you do not have one, it is perfectly fine.

Self-Love is a personal journey; we can take different paths but ultimately, we're all on the same road . There are individual ways to build self-love because the right way and the wrong way are subjective here: everyone is on a different path, but there is a single fundamental instrumental tool that can help you to change your self-talk and improve your self-love. I'm talking about journaling; this tool can help you to combat all the negative self-talk that runs on the default apps of your brain. This will not be a "magical" instant process; it will take time and you will have to work on it a lot, but you will be really surprised when you finally love yourself. This means taking a bunch of really small steps to communicate that you really care about yourself.

Women are capable of getting what they want out of life. As women, we're conditioned to be self-conscious and overly critical of our looks. Our brains are hardwired to believe that our worth is tied to how we look. To overcome this, we need to boost our self-confidence.

We are our own worst critics, and we compare ourselves to others in everything we do. It's a normal thing to do, but it can be negative when it leads to self-doubt and a feeling that you're not good enough. Women worry about many things, but this is the primary thing that women all over the world are worried about.

This book will help you to improve your self- love, happiness and positivity. However, actually implementing it in life is a task for you to do. Once you achieve everything, it changes your life forever: you start seeing good in the bad, happiness in the sadness, positive in the negatives; which ultimately makes you a calmer and better person in life.

Loving ourselves has many benefits, from an increase of self-esteem to a boost of confidence. Simply put, self-love is treating ourselves similarly to the way we treat someone else that we love, even if sometimes it is difficult for us to treat ourselves in the same way that we treat the friends we love.

A part of self-love includes understanding how our identity forms and accepting our bodies. That's why you will find a chapter about these things inside this book.

This workbook will allow you to pinpoint the key areas of your life that you need to focus on now. Life is always changing and there are always going to be areas of your life that you're trying to focus on to get better in; but self-love is a great place to start.

Once you have gotten rid of your negative self-talk, and have increased your self-confidence and self-love, you will open up a whole new world. You will spend less time worrying about things you cannot control (like why someone may not like you as much as you like them) and concentrate on those people that are in your life and love you as you are. Self-confidence and self-love will open doors that you never knew were there. Maybe you will succeed at getting the promotion that always evaded you; maybe you will find true, unconditional love; maybe you will just appreciate all you have more than ever before. However, it changes you, it will change you for the better. This workbook was written to help women to realize their best potential, realize they are worthy of self-love and unconditional love, and that they are powerful and respected.

My hope for you is that after you work through this book you will find yourself more confident, brave, and have higher self-esteem, self-love and self-confidence. There are no right or wrong answers here ... Be honest and truthful in your responses. If you do, you will have the confidence and drive to achieve anything you want in life.

CHAPTER 1
SELF-ESTEEM

In a very clinical sense, Self-esteem means how much we feel good or bad about ourselves, and that carries over to how we determine our worth and how we feel about ourselves as a person.

In another way, Webster defines self-esteem as "the holding of a good opinion of oneself," a very simple, straight-forward definition but it only scratches the surface of a complex topic that has generated a multitude of theories that are confusing and conflicting. Self-esteem is an ever-changing set of a person's attitudes about their values. We will focus on the "ever-changing part."

A renowned psychologist named William James (interestingly the brother of the famous author Henry James) used the word "self-esteem" in The Principles of Psychology, published in 1890. As James, who is often referred to as the "Father of Psychology", continued to grow prominent, so did the term self-esteem. As a concept, self-esteem continued to be used in James' theories throughout his 40-year career at Harvard, and slowly gained legitimacy. By the time of William James' death in 1910, the term self-esteem had been widely accepted throughout the mental health community.

Assigning the nomenclature is the easy part but understanding the many layers of the self-esteem topic is difficult. It is thought by some to be as straight-forward as having a three-part definition. First, in terms of success or competence, and second, feeling good about oneself or worthwhile. These are the common definitions. A third, less common definition is the "relationship" between the first and second. It makes sense that the three separate meanings can be synergistic, that is to say, work together. The relationship between feeling competent and then good about oneself would keep the other two in check, not allowing for extremes. For example, a successful CEO can be competent but have bullied his way to the top. A person can feel good emotionally and mentally but may not be able to handle social situations or intimacy. There can be extremes, even in the world of high self-esteem. Whatever definition applies, self-esteem is real and life altering. If left unattended, extremely high, exaggerated self-esteem can actually be damaging. However, the resolution of this book is to impart knowledge, to provide you with practical tools to use on your journey, and to give you hope.

There are as many reasons for the onset and existence of low self-esteem as there are people who struggle with it. Reasons can include significant, unresolved childhood issues, emotional trauma later in life, health problems, relationship problems, substance abuse, obesity, severe phobias, sleep disorders, death of loved ones, and a string of "failures." The list is endless.

There is one root cause that is found to be very prevalent in those struggling with low self-esteem, and that is childhood or early development trauma. It deserves our sharing a little more information. These traumas often involve sexual abuse, emotional abuse, physical abuse, neglect, or being separated from parents, just to name a few. These issues are very difficult to face and are painful. Also, survivors of childhood traumas often feel as if they live in a frightening world and have no control over their lives, even as adults.

Of course, low self-esteem and various types of mental illness go hand-in-hand, specifically depression. However, even challenges such as depression can be managed more effectively by implementing many of the tools we use to build self-esteem. Individuals with high self-esteem and inner-strength are less likely to be depressed or are better able to manage it.

Traumas have to be relived to some degree in order to take away their power and allow your inner strength to protect you. Facing the past and coming through the experience makes for a stronger person with greater self-esteem. These are in some ways the most difficult challenges to overcome when working on building self-esteem and mental strength. Those memories are fertile ground for negativity to creep into your thoughts. However, gaining freedom from the power of those memories leaves you free to grow into the person you have the potential to be. This workbook will provide you with some information and practical guidance to help you through that difficult process.

Another factor that can have a marked impact on self-esteem is a person's physical well-being. High self-esteem serves as a layer of protection between poor health and stress. Stress has been proven to affect all sorts of neurological functions, which in turn affect us physically and, in time, can take a real toll. This is something to keep in mind as you begin your work. It is a reminder that making a commitment to stay as healthy as you can, within your particular limits and circumstances, is very important as you work toward healthy emotions.

Someone who struggles with low self-esteem has a close relationship with an inner voice called the "Critic." A constant negative voice saying, "you can't", "you're too weak", "too dumb", "too whatever." The Critic must be met head on. Later in the book, we will address the Critic in detail and give you some practical methods to keep your Critic at bay and not controlling your life. Examples of this would be changing negative thoughts to positive ones, such as changing "limiting" to "empowering", and "I hope" to "I'm committed," or "I can't" to "I choose not to." Also, with low self-esteem, your relationships of every type will suffer. You will struggle to think of goals for your life, much less achieve them. So, you see the hard work ahead. Distinguish that you are not alone in this voyage. Others have been down the path and found their way; you can do the same. Again, you will be given some useful tools. They will help to strengthen you mentally and emotionally. Or, to quote Kierkegaard, "to be that self which one truly is."

How Self-Esteem Can Be Affected by All Media, Including Social Media

This is such an important and salient topic for today, that it is fitting for some information about it to be included in this book. Where can we go to escape magazines, television and radio and of course the all-powerful internet? I'd venture almost nowhere. We are inundated with more information than anyone can process. We cannot separate the truth from lies, what's important and what's not. It comes from so many sources, good and bad, like the entertainment industry, advertising, educational field, and government, just to name a few. It is essential to our very being that it impacts our lives, like it or not. Most of us do not have the extravagance of living on a tropical island in the South Pacific away from it all. All of this data that is thrown at us requires processing and we can't help but internalize it

Advertising is the worst. We distinguish that what we are seeing is usually misrepresented, but nevertheless we see it, buy it and talk to our friends about how awesome it is! We wouldn't want to admit that we just wasted a large sum of money on something that is really ugly and overpriced. They've given us this false picture of the US. What we should look and act like. Again, we see something we like, or how we think we should look, and we beat ourselves up when we cannot meet those expectations.

Social media have a firm grip on a portion of our lives. Even if you do not participate, you are still affected by them. They are woven into the fabric of everyday living across the globe. Can they have an effect on your self-esteem? We all know the answer. The posts run from horribly cruel to the most innocuous. We all can admit it is addictive, but it is also insidious. For an individual with low self-esteem, it seems a perfect way to stay in a safe protected world.

A person can post what they want about their life, and see the outside world only through the apps, all without setting foot out of their home. Doesn't do much for one's self esteem, does it? It can actually lead to paranoia and anxiety. You are not going to feel supported or validated by participating in a 'tweet storm'. For someone struggling with self-esteem issues, social media should be used in moderation, for recreation only and not as a primary source of communication. Don't get caught up in a social media trap.

EXERCISES

What opinion do you have of yourself ?

_____

_____

_____

_____

_____

_____

_____

Why do you think you view yourself this way?

_____

_____

_____

_____

_____

_____

How often do you speak with your "inner critic" and what does it usually tell you?

_____

_____

_____

_____

_____

_____

How do you feel after you use social media? How does it affect your self-esteem?

_____

_____

_____

_____

_____

_____

Think about a person you admire. What qualities do you share with them?

_____

_____

_____

_____

_____

Write about the last time you were proud of yourself

_____

_____

_____

_____

_____

_____

Write about your greatest talent

_____

_____

_____

_____

_____

_____

Write down an episode in your life where you overcame a fear ✎

_____

_____

_____

_____

_____

_____

Write your favorite affirmations. What do they mean to you? ✎

_____

_____

_____

_____

_____

_____

What is the best compliment you have received?

_____

_____

_____

_____

_____

_____

Do you agree with this compliment? Why ?

_____

_____

_____

_____

_____

_____

CHAPTER 2
SELF-ACCEPTANCE

My Unique Gifts

An important part of fully embracing yourself involves knowing your gifts, talents, and strengths. Sometimes others' feedback can give us evidence to support our newfound self-appreciation. In the gift pictured here, fill in things that you love about yourself. Don't be shy. Remember, you are a gift!

List six unique gifts you possess:

Things That Make Me Smile

An important component of embracing yourself is fully knowing yourself. While recognizing our gifts is essential, so too is knowing what makes us smile. In order to practice self-love, it helps to know what brings us happiness.

Fill in the heart with a few of those things. Consider nature, people, animals, ideas, and experiences. They could be small things, like making your favorite tea every morning or taking your dog for a walk.

Love Your Quirks

Part of embracing ourselves is knowing and accepting our flaws and imperfections. Imagine the power that comes from allowing ourselves to be perfectly imperfect and still know our worth. The world becomes limitless in all we can do and experience when we operate from a place of acceptance and humor, with a mindset that embraces learning and growing. Sometimes hard-learned lessons leave scars and imperfections long after the fact, and that's okay. Embracing our imperfections and quirks is an important step toward fully loving ourselves.

List six quirks or imperfections that make you special

Things I Am Thankful for On This Voyage

Gratitude has the power to transform our perspective and improve moments of pain and suffering. Learning to find gratitude in our experiences humbles us as we grow and accept lessons along our journey. Make a list of five things that you feel grateful for as you fully embrace this self-love experience.

What are five things you are grateful for?

Embracing Myself

Part of fully loving ourselves, involves treating ourselves kindly and wisely. Think of ways that you do this within your established boundaries.

Fill in the lines provided with examples of ways you embrace taking care of yourself.

Physically

_____

_____

_____

_____

_____

_____

Emotionally

_____

_____

_____

_____

_____

Financially

_____

_____

_____

_____

Mentally

_____

_____

_____

_____

Socially

_____

_____

_____

_____

Visualize Your Future Self

In the following exercise, let's visualize the older, even wiser you:

1. Close your eyes. Then take a deep breath by inhaling through your nose and exhaling through your mouth.

2. Think about what you long for in your life. Picture what it would take to have this dream come true.

3. Consider: in what ways are you limiting yourself? What blocks you from moving forward?

4. Imagine yourself dealing with and addressing these barriers. Visualize yourself overcoming and propelling yourself forward, closer to your dreams.

5. Imagine an older, wiser, and more evolved version of yourself reaching out to embrace you. Picture this version of yourself expressing appreciation and recognition for all you have accomplished so far. Picture your wise, older self-expressing gratitude for your strength and gifts.

6. Fully embrace yourself in this present moment and know that your future self will be with you along the way.

Self-Compassion Troubleshooting

When doing self-exploration activities, it's always helpful to assess and evaluate what works and doesn't work well. In these next series of exercises, we'll take some time to reflect on the core components of our self-love practice: to identify any areas that were difficult and come up with possible adjustments or improvements specific to your individual journey.

Reflect for a moment on your self-compassion practice when using this workbook. What was helpful in these exercises? What did you find challenging? Take some time to identify and list any barriers to fully embracing self-compassion. In the space after this, think about some possible solutions. This is a brainstorming assembly, so there are no wrong ideas. Go ahead and express yourself.

What worked for me

_____

_____

_____

_____

_____

_____

_____

_____

_____

Challenges in practicing self-compassion

_____

_____

_____

_____

_____

_____

Ideas and ways to improve

_____

_____

_____

_____

_____

_____

Mindfulness Troubleshooting

Mindfulness, a core component in the self-love journey, weaves throughout all of the exercises in this book. As you develop a strong ability to practice mindfulness, your efforts can prove life-changing by giving you the ability to live life in the moment, free from judgment and worries. What is more, mindfulness teaches us to accept and notice, to simply be. In doing so, we connect with the earth, the air, and all that exists around and within us. We become part of the bigger picture and realize how perfectly we fit within it.

What worked for me in these exercises

_____

_____

_____

_____

_____

_____

_____

_____

_____

I faced these challenges in practicing mindfulness during this experience

_____

_____

_____

_____

_____

_____

Ideas and ways to improve in practicing mindfulness in the future

_____

_____

_____

_____

_____

_____

Five Ways to Take Control

As we build upon practicing self-compassion, releasing self-doubt, setting boundaries, and having healthier relationships, we can consider our options—this empowers us to take control of our lives. We have several options for how we can respond to challenges that come our way. Here are five options for how we might choose to approach and handle problems in our lives. These steps all involve acknowledging and accepting situations before we can take action.

(1) Change the situation. Often, we can change a situation by expressing our wants and desires and communicating our preferences. While we might not always be able to alter the circumstances since we don't control others' feelings, thoughts, and actions, we know that to change something, we must take action.

(2) Tolerate the situation. This option involves accepting and then learning to deal with things the way they are through various coping skills and perspective-taking strategies. Of course, tolerating is not synonymous with liking—it may involve circling back after a while to decide if it's time for a change.

(3) Accept the situation. In all reality, to change and to tolerate requires acceptance. However, this option of accepting the situation embraces the struggle or potential discomfort of accepting events that we cannot change. Acceptance allows for a sort of peace and requires strong mindfulness skills. It can feel empowering to accept something that can't be changed.

(4) Do nothing. This option is simple. Do not respond to or address the situation. Ignore it completely. It's not quite the same as acceptance, since doing nothing means not working toward acceptance. For anyone who has tried to accept a situation, you know it can feel like work!

(5) Make it worse. Hopefully, you will not end up choosing this option. Making situations worse creates short- and long-term consequences in our lives and relationships. It can create chaos and unnecessary drama.

Identify a current situation that is weighing on you. Choose one of the five life options and write about what this response might look like in your situation. Is it the best choice?

_____

_____

_____

Comfort Zone

When we have the courage to reach out beyond our fears and take steps toward our goals, that is where living fully begins. Once you've embraced self-love, your life will continue to expand. The possibilities are endless. In this exercise, in the smaller inside circle, identify situations and people with whom you feel comfortable and safe. In the next circle, identify some of your limiting beliefs and insecurities. And in the third, outer circle, list all the possibilities for your growth and dreams.

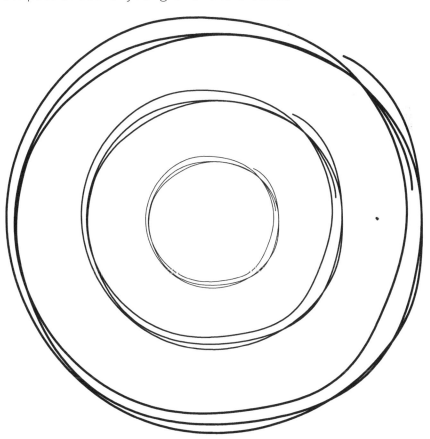

A Work in Progress

The journey toward self-love is never-ending - we will continually grow and change throughout different developmental stages in our lives and family life cycles. This workbook can be used many times throughout your life journey and can serve as a resource for years to come. In the space provided, identify three areas in which you feel you still need to grow, improve, and expand. Try setting a prompt in your calendar to check in with yourself every six months to see how you are doing with your self-love practice.

_____

_____

_____

Learning About Myself

Self-exploration can feel heavy and intense at times. When we become vulnerable and honest with ourselves, we open the door for insight and awareness to shine a light on our darkest places. Hopefully, through this workbook, you are learning a lot about yourself. Take a moment and share here how you have grown personally in completing these activities

_____

_____

_____

_____

_____

_____

Who Are Your Heroines?

As we reminisce into history, we see countless, empowering examples of strong, courageous women who embraced self-love and change wholeheartedly. Here are some examples of women and girls, real and imagined, who represent the power of self-love. Which ones do you admire or want to be like? Feel free to list your own personal heroines.

- Malala Yousafzai
- Rosa Parks
- Maya Angelou
- Helen Keller
- Annie Easley
- Jo March
- Harriet Tubman
- Anne Frank
- Saint Teresa of Calcutta
- Sojourner Truth
- Katniss Everdeen
- Merida from Brave
- Wonder Woman

_____

_____

_____

_____

_____

_____

_____

What is it about these women that motivates you?

_____

_____

_____

My Legacy

Reflection is a special and vital part of your development. Reflecting on the meaning of life offers a powerful opportunity to look deep within. Sometimes reviewing our lives allows us to consider our value and purpose. This process helps us to find meaning with which we can align our life choices and decisions, both looking back and going forward. If you were to leave a legacy behind in the world, what difference would you like to have made? Consider ways in which you can move toward a life filled with meaning and purpose. It is here, in this space, that your self-love will shine the brightest.

What will be your legacy that you leave behind?

_____

_____

_____

_____

_____

How will you work towards building the road to that legacy?

_____

_____

_____

_____

_____

Self-Love Calendar

Now that you have an assembly of activities for practicing self-love, try one skill a day using the calendar provided. Feel free to adapt with your own ideas, too!

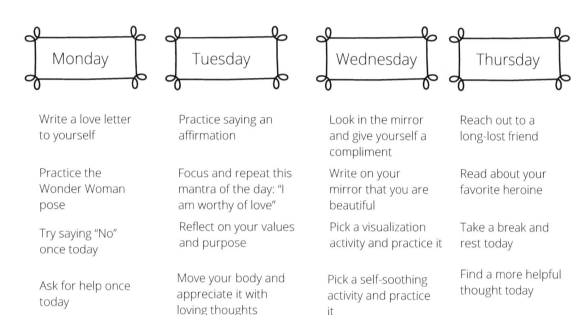

Monday

Write a love letter to yourself

Practice the Wonder Woman pose

Try saying "No" once today

Ask for help once today

Tuesday

Practice saying an affirmation

Focus and repeat this mantra of the day: "I am worthy of love"

Reflect on your values and purpose

Move your body and appreciate it with loving thoughts

Wednesday

Look in the mirror and give yourself a compliment

Write on your mirror that you are beautiful

Pick a visualization activity and practice it

Pick a self-soothing activity and practice it

Thursday

Reach out to a long-lost friend

Read about your favorite heroine

Take a break and rest today

Find a more helpful thought today

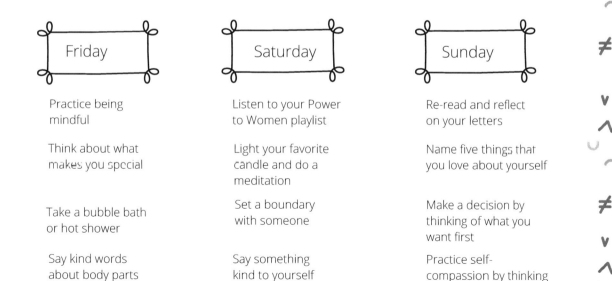

Friday

Practice being mindful

Think about what makes you special

Take a bubble bath or hot shower

Say kind words about body parts you dislike

Saturday

Listen to your Power to Women playlist

Light your favorite candle and do a meditation

Set a boundary with someone

Say something kind to yourself

Sunday

Re-read and reflect on your letters

Name five things that you love about yourself

Make a decision by thinking of what you want first

Practice self-compassion by thinking how others are like you

You Rock!

Complete the following letter of appreciation for your hard work, dedication, and willingness to explore self-love. This kind of work can feel uncomfortable and challenging at times. You are an amazing woman filled with many gifts and strengths, and you've taken big steps on this journey. Take a moment to express that appreciation to yourself.

Dear   (your name)   _ _ _ _ _ _ _ _ _ _

You are really awesome. I love the way you   _ _ _ _ _ _ _ _ _ _

I appreciate the way you practice self-love, thank you for taking the time to

_ _ _ _ _ _ _ _ _ _ _ _ _ _ _ _ _ _

I understand you overcame hard challenges in your life, like

_ _ _ _ _ _ _ _ _ _ _ _ _ _ _ _ _ _

I'm proud of how you overcame these difficulties:

_ _ _ _ _ _ _ _ _ _ _ _ _ _ _ _ _ _

You possess many of the qualities that many people would like to have, like

_ _ _ _ _ _ _ _ _ _ _ _ _ _ _ _ _ _

I'm fascinated that you

_ _ _ _ _ _ _ _ _ _ _ _ _ _ _ _ _ _

I'm sure you will improve your self-love by

_ _ _ _ _ _ _ _ _ _ _ _ _ _ _ _ _ _

Thank you for being so amazing. I love you.
Yours Truly,

_ _ _ _ _ _ _ _   (your name)

Five Takeaways into the Future

Write down five takeaways that you will carry with you into your life after having completed this workbook. Think about something you learned or see differently now. If you want, you can write them down on a piece of paper and pick one to focus on each day.

1 _____

_____

2 _____

_____

3 _____

_____

4 _____

_____

5 _____

_____

After reading this part, I'm sure you can agree that fully embracing who we are does not happen magically. It takes time and determination to learn to let go of lingering self-doubt and insecurities and accept our uncomfortable feelings and flaws. But as we allow ourselves to learn lessons in life and practice self-love, wonderful things can emerge: a reason for living, healthier relationships, and compassion for others and ourselves. Embracing ourselves enables us to embrace others and live fully.

Say to yourself: "I am continually growing and learning".

CHAPTER 3

SELF-CONFIDENCE

Trust will help us to grow closer to other women and to men. Trusting others, for example relatives and friends, can guarantee us that we will be assisted when we want it. It is the basis of any healthy relationship - such as the connection you have with yourself. Trusting yourself may build up your confidence, make it easier for you to make choices, and lower your stress levels. And the fantastic thing is that even in the event that you don't trust yourself today, with some effort you'll be able to develop that confidence with time.

Strategies for Building Trust on Your Own

There is no one more important to trust than yourself. Occasionally, we lose trust in ourselves if we make a mistake or following someone criticizing us constantly. It may feel more challenging to make decisions if you cannot trust yourself, as you fear you will make the wrong choice. Or you may be more likely to criticize your decisions once you make them.

Building trust on your own might help to boost your decision-making abilities and self-confidence. This will make life feel somewhat easier and considerably more enjoyable. Below are a few pointers that will support you in learning to trust yourself:

Be Yourself

Should you dread the way others will look at you or judge you, then you may find it hard to be yourself around other people. Feeling like a different person than who you are is an indication that you are lacking self-confidence and confidence on your own. Other folks are going to have the ability to feel that.

So how can you grow your confidence enough to be around other people? When you begin to feel insecure around other people, remind yourself that it is OK to be you. Begin with practicing around the people that you feel comfortable with, such as your own friends and family. Take note if you're feeling uncomfortable or vulnerable and keep spending time with these folks until your insecure emotions begin to disappear.

Once you are yourself around others, they will treat you with additional trust. This could enable you to grow your confidence in yourself.

EXERCISES

What qualities of yours can you bring to the group next time you're in a social setting?

_____

_____

_____

_____

_____

How can you ensure that you are being your true self?

_____

_____

_____

_____

_____

Establish Reasonable Goals

Frequently we aim high with all our objectives. Rather than aiming to earn $50,000 annually from our occupation, we plan to create $100,000. Rather than attempting to finish a job in a couple of weeks, we attempt to get it done in one week. And setting our targets high might be a fantastic thing, since it motivates us to work hard for what we desire.

Regrettably, setting goals which are too ambitious includes a significant downside. As soon as we do not reach our big objectives, we encounter failure. Failing often can lower your self-confidence and capacity to trust yourself.

Rather than setting one big target, try placing many small goals that put you on the path of your bigger aim. Doing this will make your big target more realistic. You will also get confidence in yourself while reaching the smaller milepost along the way.

Write down three tangible and reasonable goals that you would like to accomplish:

Be Kind to Your self

It's likely that you've heard the expression "unconditional love". Maybe it's been mentioned in connection to the relationship a parent has with their child, or even the love which exists between grandparents, friends, as well as romantic partners. But did you know that it's also tremendously important to enjoy yourself unconditionally?

Loving yourself means eliminating negative ideas about yourself and some other self-criticism when you make a mistake. Begin by keeping a close eye on your own internal voice, and the way it responds to your activities. Is it kind or mean? Is it critical or accepting? When you can love yourself, you may be prepared unreservedly, and that shapes self-confidence.

Write down five positive and kind affirmations you can say to yourself

Build on Your Strengths

Everyone is better at some things and worse in others. Now you probably have a great idea about what you excel at and what you do not do so well with. Trusting yourself implies having the ability to try to do all sorts of tasks, deprived of judging yourself too severely.

What are your strengths?

_____

_____

_____

Spend Some Time on Your Own

If you don't trust yourself, you may feel uncomfortable spending some time looking inward. You may attempt to stay busy daily by always getting involved in activities or considering little things outside of yourself. Break the habit of looking away from yourself by looking inward.

It is possible to look in with meditation. Consider sitting in a quiet location for 5 to 15 minutes every day. Pay careful attention to your body and breath. As any notions or self-criticisms pass, admit them and let them go. Allowing yourself to get this significant one-on-one time can grow your self-trust.

What can you do to spend time with yourself every day?

_____

_____

_____

Be Essential

We lack confidence in ourselves if we question our activities or decisions. Occasionally we may even wonder who we are. That may hurt.

Shape trust in yourself by stopping your practice of questioning your choices. In the time after you make a decision, stay with it. Even though it turns out subsequently not to be the ideal choice, there is no use beating yourself up over the choice you made.

The best that you could do is to learn from the error. Think of how you'll make a much better decision next time, and proceed. Doing this can allow you to learn to become more trusting of yourself, along with your decision-making abilities.

What decisions have you made that you are confident about?

_____

_____

_____

_____

_____

What decisions have you made that you would like to learn from?

_____

_____

_____

_____

_____

Write down your past career success

_____

_____

_____

_____

Write down your past family success

_____

_____

_____

_____

Write down your past sport / hobby success

_____

_____

_____

_____

List your core values for the following:

Family

_____

_____

Spiritual

_____

_____

Education

_____

_____

Career

_____

_____

Friends

_____

_____

List areas or situations where you don't feel confident.

_____

_____

_____

_____

_____

_____

Why do you feel under-confident in these scenarios? (If you have difficulty responding now, wait until you've gone through this workbook.)

_____

_____

_____

_____

_____

_____

What is one of your "flaws" you currently avoid sharing with others, or feel insecure about when it comes up?

_____

_____

_____

How could this imperfection actually make you a better person?

_____

_____

_____

How could you share this "flaw" with others in a way that was funny and demonstrated confidence?

_____

_____

_____

The Most Important Thing

Trusting yourself is among the most helpful things you can do in your life. It helps build your confidence, lets other people trust you more, and makes the process of decision-making easier. To be ready, all you need to do is to make a tiny effort, create self-love, and locate the capacity to look inward.

CHAPTER 4

OVERWHELMED THINKING

The Mind and Your Inner "What If?" Voice

In order to overcome anxiety, generalized anxiety disorder, panic attacks, phobias, and all related issues, we'll need to create new paths in the brain.

No worries, this is much easier than it sounds: you've been doing it all your life.

Do you remember that, when you were a toddler, walking was out of the question? How about riding a bike? Do you recall how impossible that appeared? What about using a hammer and a nail for the first time? These may all have been accompanied by pretty painful learning curves.

You had to put in effort and time intentionally to study how it functioned, why it worked and what the rules were. Then after days, weeks, or often months of practicing, you turned out to be better at it, up until it became automatic. You had shaped a habit and you could do it without intentionally focusing on it.

Something amazing happens when we learn a new skill. Our brain starts to form new neural pathways so that something you had to focus on consciously at first can become automated. That's pretty powerful stuff.

Your brain has only so much energy and willpower every day, and tries to become as effective and efficient as possible. In order to do so, it cuts corners.

Write about 2 skills you had to learn consciously at first but are now automatic for you:

_____

_____

_____

Everything We Repeat or Think Often Becomes Automatic

Both good and bad repetitions become automatic. Your mind makes no distinction! Nathan Spreng, a neuroscientist at Cornell University, did a scientific meta-analysis on this, together with many other scientists who have been studying the brain for decades. Whenever you repeat a process, your mind believes it must be important, so it memorizes and automates it. Can you see how essential this is?

Because you repeated being anxious, freaking out, or worrying about everything so often, your mind believes it must be very important to you. Why else would you practice it so frequently? It's probably not for fun.

So, it strengthens that pathway in your brain, making it easier for you to become anxious... automatically! I was mind blown when I first had this realization.

This, luckily, is reversible because the brain plasticity remains, no matter our age, as other interesting studies prove. And as my clients older than 80 have proven too.

Right now, whenever you have an anxious thought, your mind still habitually goes into the "what if?" mode. We'll just need to reverse that step by step, and this is much easier than you think.

Before we move on, let me prove this both to you and possibly to your negative voice that may be skeptical right now.

Please think of something you do often nowadays, without fear, while it made you anxious at first.

_____

_____

_____

For some people, it's driving their car; for others, it's swimming, riding a bike, horseback riding...

This is the usual way we conquer normal anxiety. By exposing ourselves to it over and over again, we learn that it's OK. The anxiety vanishes, and that scary thing becomes embedded into our comfort circle. We can then partake in it without fear.

Nonetheless, as I'm sure you found out, pure exposure is not enough to conquer irrational fears. For those irrational fears, we'll need to take out the heavy toolbox. And that's what part two is for.

Exactly What to Tell Yourself to Overcome Anxiety and Panic Attacks

Your internal dialogue and what you keep telling yourself plays a major role as we've seen. It is what makes the difference between feeling anxious for less than a minute, rather than developing generalized anxiety disorder, having panic attacks, or suffering from phobias.

First, imagine that you're looking after an eight-year-old girl who says, "Hey, I feel scared. I think there's a monster in my cabinet. I'm afraid."

How will you respond?

Suppose you say, "Oh my! You should be afraid! You're right. Even though monsters don't exist, there may be a burglar, a kidnapper or even a serial killer in your closet. And don't get me started about snakes and spiders... And ghosts! Even though the jury is out on those, I believe they exist. Anyway, bad things are about to happen to you either way, my dear. And it's not just your closet you should be afraid of! You have no idea how tough life will get from here on out! Don't you read the newspaper or watch the news? Life is bad. Trust me. I'm an adult. I know everything."

Can you picture the face of the little girl you've been explaining this to? Will this advice help? Of course not! You'll make her cry and scare her even more! That's obvious.
But if this is so obvious... the question is, why do anxious people talk in that exact same way to themselves? Their minds go on and on and imagine things that could indeed happen, but where the possibility of it actually occurring is less than 1%.
What kinds of things do you say to yourself when you're anxious? I'm sure it's not kind and soothing. You may also be disappointed in yourself just because you had the thoughts or the anxiety in the first place. That disappointment is harsh as well.

Imagine lashing out at the eight-year-old girl with, "Why does this always happen to you? Why are you having these fears? I'm so disappointed..." That wouldn't help either.
If you kept track of your self-talk, your inner dialogue, you'd be surprised at how badly you're often treating yourself.

Our internal dialogue during moments of intense anxiety would often be classified as verbal abuse should we use the same language outwardly towards others!
If a real eight-year-old sought your reassurance, I'm sure you would calm the little girl down and say kind things. And that's what you'll need to do with yourself. Self-compassion is crucial!

At every moment of the day while you're awake, you're talking to yourself, all the time. And the road you pick will strongly color your mood, your feelings, your stress level, and of course, your anxiety level.

If you react badly to one negative thought, you'll probably still feel fine. Yet when you keep reacting negatively, you're setting yourself up for constant anxiety.

Recount two episodes where your internal dialogue exacerbated your irrational fears and anxiety:

_____

_____

_____

_____

_____

You Get to Decide How You Answer to Every Event That Happens in Your Life.

Anxiety is a choice.

It took me a long time to admit this. How could it possibly be a choice? I didn't want the anxiety.

We don't always choose our initial reaction, but we do choose the reaction to that first layer of anxiety. This is called emotional intelligence. We have the power to make an intelligent choice about the thoughts we use and thus the emotions we feel.

Neurologist and psychiatrist Victor Frankl, the man who not only survived the Nazi death camps but even learned how to have fun while being in the most horrendous place on earth at that time, went on to perfect this.

If you let your thoughts lead the way, you're living your life in a reactive state, and you'll never feel like you are in control.

Easier said than done, of course. I'm sure you have tried to think positive as many gurus always proclaim; but that never works for long or sometimes not even at all.

So, what can you do then when you are minding your own business, and a what-if thought pops up or anything else that makes you anxious?

Step one is to question those negative thoughts.

Counterintuitive Questions You Can Use When You're Anxious

Thinking in a non-anxious way is like trying to pick up the heavy weights in the gym you cannot lift yet. In what way do you get to a point where you can lift them up with relative ease? You start with lighter weights, you train, and you allow the muscle to grow and become stronger.

That's what you'll need to do with your mind as well. Train it, and it will become stronger!

As a first step, I would like to ask you to question your own negative thoughts whenever you have them. Whenever something scares you and gives you the anxiety you're trying to leave behind, analyze what you had just been thinking. Observe what your mind comes up with.

What was the first domino? What thought led you to having the anxiety? What thought triggered it?

Please realize it will have been a thought. It's not the location, the thing you saw, the sensation you felt, or the people you're with that gave you the anxiety. It will have been a thought that you had as a reaction to what happened. What was your thought? Write it down as soon as you can afterward.

When you have good anxiety, like the anxiety you'll feel when you see a tarantula bathing itself in your bathtub, it will be caused by an instinctive reaction led by your amygdala, the part of your brain that instantly decides whether something is a threat or not.

With bad anxiety, it will most often be a thought that starts with, "Oh no, what if?" or "What will people think if?" or "What's this symptom I'm feeling?" etc.

For the next couple of days, I would like you to look for your trigger thoughts. What are they? What makes the first domino drop?

It often goes like this:
• You see something > thought and anxiety trigger > anxiety
• You feel something > thought and anxiety trigger > anxiety
• You see someone > thought and anxiety trigger > anxiety

I admit there are exceptions to this rule. It can happen that you've had a serious bout of anxiety in a certain location and being in the same or a similar place gives you the initial feeling of anxiety. That's because your mind remembered how seemingly life-threatening your previous experience was and wants you to avoid it.

Every time we panic like a maniac or act like a bloodthirsty tiger has just started to lick our legs, our brain remembers the exact setting this horrendous event took place in. It will do everything it can to have you avoid it the next time.

Thinking about it will be enough to launch all of the symptoms. But even then, they are still thoughts that will raise the anxiety level and potentially start the vicious cycle.

For the next couple of days, please write down your trigger thoughts. The ones you've had right before the anxiety rose significantly.

As soon as you have pinpointed your trigger thoughts, question them. Ask questions like "Is it really that bad?" and "Is this really that life threatening that I have to respond as if I'm surrounded by hungry tigers who've been fed a vegan diet for months?" and "Am I really in trouble?" and "Do I really have a problem, right now, in this present moment?" Question their validity. Question whether the anxiety system that had been launched was really needed to come to a solution. It wasn't, if you weren't in any real, imminent, physical danger.

Questioning negative thoughts takes away their power, as you'll start to discover.

Trigger thought 1

_____

_____

_____

Trigger thought 2

_____

_____

_____

Trigger thought 3

_____

_____

_____

CHAPTER 5

ANXIETY

What Is Anxiety?

Anxiety is a reaction of agitation, such as discomfort or fright, that can be slight or grave. Each person has moods of anxiety during times in their life. Falling in love and being in love challenges us in various and numerous ways. A number of these challenges are unexpected, and when we face them for the first time, our human nature makes us defensive. For example, if you love somebody without question, and he or she makes you extremely upset, odds are, you will not try to be defenseless. On an individual point, we all dread being hurt deliberately, or unknowingly. Unexpectedly, this dread rises up when we are making plans. At the slightest possibility that a relationship is acceptable, one begins to fear the 'effect of a separation.' Consequently, one begins to protect oneself, make a separation, and cut off the association in the long run. If we are encountering love and being treated in an uncommonly decent manner, we become tense.

That defensive tension becomes a barrier. It is important to note that anxiety in a relationship does not only arise because of the things going on between the two parties involved. This feeling may also arise because of our perception. The things you tell yourself about a relationship, love, attraction, desire, etcetera will affect your life. This means that you might have the best partner in the world, but your thoughts still hinder you from realizing it, and enjoying the moment. The proverbial 'inner voice' is very dangerous if it is negative. This mental coach can tell us things that fuel our fear of intimacy. The critical inner voice can feed us lousy advice such as: "You are too ugly for him/her", "Other people have left you before", and "You cannot trust such a man/woman".

What do such thoughts do? They make us turn against the people we love and, most importantly, ourselves. The critical inner voice can make us hostile, paranoid, and unnecessarily suspicious. It can also drive our feelings of defensiveness, distrust, anxiety, and jealousy to unhealthy levels. This tiny negative voice feeds us an endless stream of unhealthy thoughts that make us worried about relationships and undermine our happiness. It prevents us from enjoying life wholesomely.

The main challenge comes once we focus on these thoughts. We get into our heads and focus on whatever that minute thought is saying. Then we process it, ponder it, and roast and re-roast it - until it appears like an unmovable mountain. At that moment, one is distracted from one's partner, thus there can be no real relation and interaction. After brewing over the thoughts, one might start to act out, either immaturely or in destructive ways. For instance, one might start to boss one's partner around, monitoring all his or her moves, making unnecessary, nasty comments, ignoring, or mistreating the other.

Suppose your partner stays late at work or passes by the local bar for a drink before coming home. The critical inner voice will trigger thoughts such as: "Where is he/she?", "What is he doing, with who and why?"; "Does she/he prefer to be away from home?", "Maybe he/she doesn't love me any more". These opinions can run through your mind so much that by the time your partner gets home, you are feeling completely insecure, paranoid, furious, and defensive. In this state, it becomes hard to have a constructive conversation about his or her whereabouts. Consequently, this partner will feel misunderstood and frustrated. Furthermore, he or she will also take a defensive stance. Soon, the dynamic of the relationship shifts from pleasure and comfort, to irrational and unfair treatments; instead of enjoying the rest of the evening, it becomes wasted as everyone feels withdrawn and upset. Do you realize that in such a case, you have effectively created the distance you initially feared? You also realize that your partner might have had no harmful intentions. The fact is the distance you have created was not caused by the situation itself, or circumstances. No. It was triggered by that critical inner voice, which might have been wrong. That voice colored your thinking with negativity, distorted your perception, and in the end, led you to self-destruction.

The biggest challenge that leads us to self-destruction in relationships is self-doubt. If we assess most of the things we worry about in a relationship, we realize that we can handle the consequences. The majority of us are resilient enough to experience heartbreaks and heal. It has probably happened before, and you didn't die from it. However, our inner voice tends to blow things out of proportion, especially the negative ones. That voice terrorizes and catastrophizes everything, making it hard to stay rational. It can trigger severe anxiety spells over some non-existent relationship dynamics and strange, intangible threats. Probably, breakups wouldn't be so painful if we didn't have that critical voice. It is the influence that analyzes things, and tears us apart by pointing out all our flaws and things we failed to do. The distorted reality makes us think that we are not healthy and resilient enough to survive. That critical voice is the cynical friend who is always giving bad advice: "You cannot survive a heartbreak; just stay guarded and do not become vulnerable."

We form our defenses based on unique life-experiences and adaptations. The inner voice also borrows from those unique experiences. If a former partner said that he or she would leave you because you are overweight or underweight, the inner voice would use that line to distort reality. It will make you think that another partner is noticing the same flaws, and that he or she will leave because of them. When feeling insecure or anxious, some of us tend to become desperate, or clingy in our actions. Others become control freaks, wanting to possess their partners. Many people start to feel crowded, as if there is no breathing space in the relationship, thus choosing to distance themselves from their loved ones.

In extreme cases, we detach from the feelings of desire in the relationship. We can start to be aloof, guarded, or wholly withdrawn. Such patterns of attachment and relating can come from our early life experiences. In childhood years, we develop attachment patterns unconsciously, depending on our environment. The patterns become the model for our adult life. They influence how we assess our needs and how we get them fulfilled. These attachment patterns and styles are the main determinants of the anxiety one feels in a relationship.

Understanding the difference between normal sensations of anxiety and an anxiety disorder calling for clinical attention can help individuals to identify and treat the problem. Everybody feels distressed now and then. It's a normal emotion. For example, you may feel worried when faced with trouble at the office, before taking a test, or making a vital choice.

Stress and anxiety conditions are different, though. They are a group of mental diseases, and the distress they trigger can keep you from carrying on with your life regularly. For individuals who have such a condition, worry and anxiety are constant and frustrating and can be disabling. However, with therapy, many individuals can take care of those sensations and get back to a satisfying life. Of course, when a normal individual encounters possibly harmful or distressing triggers, feelings of stress and anxiety are not just typical but necessary for survival.

Since the earliest days of humankind, the danger of predators and incoming threats trigger alarms in the body and permit incredibly elusive activity. These alarm systems become noticeable in the form of an elevated heartbeat, sweating, and a boosted level of sensitivity to environments. The risk brings a rush of adrenalin, a hormone and chemical messenger in the mind, which triggers these anxious responses in a procedure called the 'fight-or-flight' reaction. This prepares people physically to confront or leave any type of potential hazards to safety and security.

For many individuals, hazards ranging from bigger animals to snakes, and any impending natural threat, are a much less important issue than they would have been for very early human beings. Stress and anxieties currently revolve around the job, cash, domesticity, wellness, and other important issues that demand a person's focus, but without always calling for the 'fight-or-flight' response.

Before a vital life occasion or throughout a difficult situation, the anxious sensation is an all-natural echo of the initial 'fight-or-flight' reaction. It can still be essential to survival-- anxiety about being struck by a car when crossing the street, as an example, means that an individual will naturally look both ways to avoid the threat.

Stress and anxiety are your body's all-natural reactions to stressful situations. It's a sensation of concern or worry concerning what's ahead. Going to a job interview or providing a speech might trigger many people to feel scared and worried about the first day at work, or the public function. Yet if your feelings of stress and anxiety are severe, last for longer than six months, and are hindering your life, you might have an anxiety condition.

The period or extent of a distressed feeling can, in some cases, be out of proportion to the original trigger or stress factor. Physical signs and symptoms, such as raised blood pressure as well as nausea, may also develop. These responses move beyond stress and anxiety, into a stress and anxiety condition. The APA defines an individual with an anxiety disorder as "having persisting invasive thoughts or problems". As soon as stress and anxiety get to the disease stage, they can hinder daily functioning.

It's typical to feel distressed about transferring to a brand-new area, beginning a brand-new job, or taking a test. This sort of tension is unpleasant. However, it might rouse you to work more thoroughly and thus improve your work. Normal nervousness is an sensation that reoccurs: nonetheless, it doesn't meddle with your regular day-to-day existence. When it comes to an anxiousness condition, the feeling of fear may be with you at all times. It is intense and also often crippling.

This kind of anxiety may trigger you to stop doing things you appreciate. It might prevent you from going into an elevator, going across the street, or even leaving your home in extreme cases. If left neglected, the anxiety will undoubtedly keep getting worse. Anxiousness problems are one of the most usual types of mental illness and can influence any person at any age. Concurring to the American Psychiatric Organization, ladies are more likely than men to be identified with an anxiousness problem.

EXERCISES

List some intrusive thoughts that repeatedly make you anxious

_____

_____

_____

_____

How secure or insecure are you in a relationship? Why?

_____

_____

_____

_____

How do you deal with anxiety in relationships?

_____

_____

_____

_____

How do you behave or react when you are feeling extremely anxious?

_____

_____

_____

_____

_____

How do you get yourself to calm down from an anxiety attack?

_____

_____

_____

_____

Write down 5 lessons you've learned from anxiety

_____

_____

_____

_____

_____

Write down three positive things that happened to you recently: be as detailed as possible.

_____

_____

_____

_____

_____

Describe how you feel right now: be as detailed as possible

_____

_____

_____

_____

Write down a list of questions that are often running through your head

_____

_____

_____

_____

Try to answer the questions you wrote before

_____

_____

_____

_____

_____

Is there someone, in particular, that is causing you anxiety? Write them a letter that you never intend to send. Get your thoughts out.

_____

_____

_____

_____

Write down what scares you the most and try to explain why

_____

_____

_____

_____

Write down your favorite memories from childhood. You may find that this "look-back" helps you to handle anxiety.

_____

_____

_____

_____

Look back to the past and write about the time when you were experiencing the most anxiety. Describe how you overcame that anxiety. Write how you will cope with anxiety in the future.

_____

_____

_____

_____

_____

Write down a moment that made you smile today. Reflect on that moment

_____

_____

_____

What song makes you feel happy? Describe why you love this song so much

_____

_____

_____

_____

_____

Try to describe your anxiety as an imaginary monster and write a short story about it

_____

_____

_____

_____

From now, I'll let go of things I can't control, including ...

_____

_____

_____

_____

CHAPTER 6

DEPRESSION

The Definition of Depression

Depression has long been a subject of fascination for medical professionals, all the way from speculations about the illness of the painter Vincent Van Gogh, to interest in celebrities and the fine points of their private lives. Depression is a common subject both for literature and discussion. In spite of all this apparent talk about depressive illness, men and women often have difficulty recognizing it in those around them, or even in themselves. This makes depression a complex "bag of worms", something tricky and elusive.

Part of what makes depression so difficult for people to understand is the assumption of knowledge that many people have about depression. Many people experience periods of being down or low in their lives, and they believe that this places them in a position to understand depression in others. But sadness can take many forms. Sadness can manifest differently in different people. What presented in one person as a day or two of lying in bed because of a bad breakup, may be a completely different experience in someone else's life. A depressed person may be withdrawn from others, or they may lash out. They may abstain from eating, or they may go on a drinking binge.

Because sadness can manifest in a variety of ways, it is easy for people to feel that they understand depression when really they do not. What one person experiences may have been a brief episode that was not significantly disturbing and was quickly resolved; yet it can be truly debilitating in another person. It is typical for people to project their own perceptions onto other people. In the case of depressive illness, this means that some do not recognize the seriousness of depression because of their own experiences with it. It is important not to do this because every person is unique: having a unique collection of thoughts and experiences characteristic of them alone.

Sadness can be extremely serious. It is believed that at least half of all people who commit suicide experience a major depressive disorder. Suicide is a grave problem globally, especially in a Western developed world where rates tend to be much higher than in "undeveloped" or "underdeveloped" countries. Although the reasons for this are up for debate, there is an active discussion about why this discrepancy in suicide rates might exist. This and other interesting aspects of depression render this an active subject of study, in spite of the century or more of study that has already taken place.

One of the most important factors to note about depressive illness, especially in the context of this book, is that depression does not merely impact the depressed individual. Sadness can also have a significant impact on others around that person. This is something that the reader is likely to know, as you made the decision to pick up a book about understanding depression in the context of a relationship. A depressed individual has the same needs that others have when it comes to the basic needs of life, income, love, relationships, and everything else, but being depressed can impact the ability of individuals to function and to meet those needs.

From the standpoint of a relationship, a depressed individual may have difficulty forming or maintaining a relationship. A depressed person may be withdrawn or otherwise does not communicate, and this may render it more difficult for them to form relationships as easily as others. If the depressed individual is already in a relationship, their partner may find them very difficult to deal with when they are in the midst of a depressive episode. This makes maintaining relationships hard, but it also gives the significant other an opportunity to be the 'life-vest' that their partner needs. A significant other who understands depression, and how to manage it, can help to alleviate the depression of their partner; which can not only save the relationship but in reality, it may actually save that person's life.

In fact, the suicide risk that people often associate with sadness is just a small part of the complex quilt that depression represents. Individuals with major depressive disorder experience significant dysfunction in their lives, and these dysfunctional states can drag on for years as the person cycles in and out of melancholic depression. A person can live a life with little or no joy for decades - which for some people causes so much misery that they describe it as being worse than death. Part of helping someone with sadness may involve helping them out of the quagmire that a lifetime of depression represents.

The low mood and lack of interest (called "anhedonia" by professionals) that people associate with sadness are important, but they are just a part of the complex picture of depression. As anyone who is in a relationship with a depressed individual knows, not only can sadness look different in different people, but it can look different in the same person from one day to the next. Understanding depression requires learning what sadness can look like in all its various forms, and knowing how to diagnose it.

The Mystique Surrounding Depression

There has been a measure of romanticism surrounding depression throughout the centuries. Individuals with an artistic inclination were often described as melancholic or depressed. This designation almost diminishes the importance of depression by suggesting that it is a flight of fancy, a passion that comes and goes and rarely leaves a mark. This is especially true in European tradition, though the same may be said of other countries. Many figures of literary or historical importance were known to experience depressive episodes. Indeed, depression was so common in some communities that some people came to regard it as a disease of artists. This state of affairs seemed to be magnified in the 19th century as cases of famous individuals suffering from depressive illness, or even dying from it, became more common.

The story of Crown Prince Rudolph of Austria is one of those stories that is sometimes mentioned, though it may be only peripherally tied to the historical narrative of depression. Crown Prince Rudolph, the only son of Emperor Franz Joseph of Austria-Hungary, committed suicide at Mayerling lodge in Austria in 1889, although conspiracy theories that he was assassinated by the Freemasons or some other group have continued to abound right up to the present. Perhaps what is significant to note about Rudolph's story is that this episode involved not only the suicide of the prince, but it also involved the death of his mistress, Mary Vetsera as well.

Historical case studies of depression help us to get a sense of how depression is tied to a human being regardless of what time they live in. Case studies are popular in psychiatry because they give the clinician and the layperson an opportunity to see how a condition can play out in the lives of "everyday people". It is easy for clinicians to approach mental illness from a clinical standpoint, without remembering that these are people not unlike themselves: people that have lives, families, lovers, and other aspects of themselves that everyone has.

This is an aspect of depressed individuals that the reader is likely to understand, because they themselves are likely to be part of the fabric of the depressed person's life. A depressed or suicidal person is not just a statistic, or news in the local newspaper. He or she is a person who has people close to them, people who may not understand the underlying issue that needs to be addressed.

Crown Prince Rudolph lived in a time of rapid social change. Although there were still monarchies in Europe, the Industrial Revolution and the societal changes that it brought along with it, as well as the rapid growth of the middle class, seemed to render men like Rudolph obsolete. Although scholars have debated why precisely Rudolph committed suicide, this idea that the prince experienced a type of situational melancholic depression that consumed his entire being is a theory that does appear to have its merit.

Like other case studies, the case of Crown Prince Rudolph leaves us with as many questions as answers. Did he suffer from depressive illness, or did he perhaps suffer from another condition? Was there a family history of depression? Was there something that his wife or those around him could have done to prevent his death at Mayerling? One thing that the reader can gain by studying Rudolph's case is the sense that depressed individuals are not all from a cookie-cutter. They do not all fall into a single demographic picture, and the question of how to handle their depression is not always a simple one. Crown Prince Rudolph may have suffered from a unique type of melancholic depression that may have been particularly difficult to handle because there were no medications at the time, and its presence did not fit the standard melancholy of the artist.

Rudolph was not alone. Austria-Hungary at the end of the 19th century was notorious for the many suicides that plagued its middle- and upper classes. Men and women often committed suicide together, jumping off of buildings, holding hands, or leaping in front of trains. Although the social factors that created this sort of context in a European nation at this time are outside the scope of this book, the connection between those days and today should be relatively apparent even to the casual observer.

Part of what makes cases like Rudolph's hard to understand is the idea that someone with seemingly so many advantages would want to commit suicide.

Not only was Rudolph the sole heir to the throne of the second largest country in Europe, but he was the beneficiary of a large royal income that permitted him to engage in whatever artistic and philosophical pastimes that were of interest to him. In a time of crushing poverty, where peasants all over Europe were leaving their homelands to seek better options in colonial nations like the United States, Canada, Australia and Brazil, the idea that someone like Rudolph would commit suicide, when so many were struggling just to survive, was alarming - and it is not difficult to understand why many are left puzzled.

Rudolph's death caused shockwaves all over Europe. As outrageous as it would have been for the crown prince and heir to the throne of a major country to die suddenly by violent means, it was unheard of for someone in Crown Prince Rudolph's position to die by suicide. Making matters worse, the death of Rudolph and Mary Vetsera was considered a murder-suicide, in which the crown prince allegedly murdered the woman he loved before he killed himself. Whatever that truth was, let me ask you to focus on your own experience again.

EXERCISES

Write down your experience with depression or depressive symptoms

_____

_____

_____

_____

What hobby you would like to start? How do you think this could make you feel better?

_____

_____

_____

_____

What area of your life are you most unhappy with? How can you start making changes to improve this area?

_____

_____

_____

_____

Write about a time you helped someone

_____

_____

_____

_____

Do you think there are negative people in your life who you should remove? How do they affect your feelings?

_____

_____

_____

_____

Are there people who have a positive impact in your life? Write about them

_____

_____

_____

_____

_____

Try to imagine your life if you were not depressed

_____

_____

_____

_____

_____

List 5 techniques you can use the next time you feel depressed.

_____

_____

_____

_____

_____

CHAPTER 7

WORRYING

How Your Brain Tells You to Freak Out

Let's talk a little neurobiology. Yay, more science! When you experience fear and worry, what is ultimately happening is that the part of your brain responsible for thinking provides feedback to the part of your brain responsible for producing emotions. This is how you determine whether you are safe or unsafe in your surroundings. Using this same communication pattern, you can be driven quickly into a heightened state, which can then turn either into fear (bad) or excitement (good).

If this communication translates into fear, this begins the worrying process in your body. When you worry, the amygdala, which is a part of your brain, is essentially letting your brain know that the sensory signals that it is interpreting are alerting for danger. This portion of your brain is responsible for letting the rest of your brain know that it can either relax; or that it needs to begin producing other necessary responses to protect you from the danger it is perceiving. Emotional memories that we experience within our lifetimes are stored with a direct connection to the center of the amygdala, which supports them in being able to determine situations that are risky. Anything that produced emotional trauma or danger in the past would be perceived as capable of producing it again in the present or future. This causes the rest of the brain to begin responding in a way that produces the hormones required to jump-start your body into action and get you ready either for fight, or flight.

And let's not forget the role that the hippocampus plays in all of this. The hippocampus is specifically responsible for your remembering threatening events and how you store them as memories so that you can prevent yourself from reliving these experiences in the real world. You can thank your hippocampus for being the reason you don't go around sticking your head in the oven every day. If you touched a hot stove when you were a child and burned yourself, your hippocampus recognizes this danger, turns it into a memory, and informs your brain that any time this danger is perceived to be risky in the future, the body must act in a certain way to prevent it.

The hippocampus tends to be smaller in individuals who experience some form of serious trauma in their lives. For example, people who were victims of abuse (especially in childhood) and people who served in combat in the military tend to have a smaller hippocampus. The reduction in size of this part of the brain may result in these particular individuals experiencing fragmented memories, particularly surrounding the trauma, which leads to their suffering flashbacks of those traumatic events. For that reason, individuals who have suffered with notable trauma in their lives are known to be at higher risk of experiencing mental distress and worry than others.

As with many things, there is a positive and a negative side. Anxiety and worry have a powerful ability to fuel the body and protect you from dangerous situations. When the body is operating healthily, these two emotions operate almost the same as stress does. The primary difference, however, is that stress is typically just felt as an overwhelming physical feeling within the body, whereas anxiety and worry can present mental distress through negative thoughts and feelings. So, say you come home after a hard day at work, and you are feeling stressed out. You may be a little overwhelmed and uncomfortable, but you are not likely to have any one particular thought entrapped in your mind. Alternatively, if you are experiencing anxiety or worry, it is likely that you are extremely focused on the world around you; and that you may be hypersensitive to various things, or obsessing over one particular thing. This will depend on whether you are experiencing anxiety or worry towards one specific situation, or in general.

Having bouts of anxiety and worry is still normal, even when they become seemingly out of control. Even perfectly healthy adults can experience panic attacks without having to be diagnosed with any form of mental or emotional disorder, or condition that would trigger the attack. These are simply chemical responses to life that happen within the brain and occasionally get beyond our control.

However, having frequent or unstoppable bouts of anxiety and worry on an ongoing basis can signal that something is wrong. While some people may genuinely need medication and professional support in finding solace from these symptoms, others might find that through mental training and strengthening they are able to find freedom from their symptoms, so that they can go on to have a healthy psyche once more.

If you find that you're having frequent bouts of anxiety or worry, or that you feel as if you're "freaking out" to an extent that it is causing severe disruption and discomfort in your life, it is time that you start taking better care of your mental health. There are numerous things that you can do to strengthen your mental health, which will not only support you in eliminating worry and anxiety, but will also support you in experiencing greater positivity in your mind. When you put in the work to eliminate problematic anxiety and stress, you are actually using tools that are powerful in helping you to silence your inner voice so that you can get back to those good vibes only. Through this, you can free yourself of the limitations bestowed upon you by the toxic "voice in your head" that loves to bring you down.

How to Eliminate Worry

So, what's the best way to eliminate worry? Be prepared to be shocked. I'm about to rock your world. We're about to go where no man has gone before... Not really. You probably won't be surprised to learn that one of the best things you can do to eradicate worry and silence your negative inner voice is meditation. Meditation is highly praised for - let's be honest, pretty much everything. It's pretty high up there right along with coconut oil, apple cider vinegar, and a Beyoncé album for being a fix-all solution. Using meditation as a way to regain control over your mind may be something you've heard before, but have you done it? Have you done it consistently? If you haven't, then let's be real—you needed to hear again about how something that, ironically, entails doing pretty much nothing can fix pretty much everything!

Meditating does not have to be some long, drawn-out ritual of candles, gongs, incense, elephant print pants and contorted cirque du soleil body positions that takes hours out of your daily life. You don't have to sell all your belongings, grow your hair to your waist, and live off the land to meditate. Although, you can certainly be that person if that is who you desire to become. Hey, I'm not judging. But in all seriousness, meditation is an incredible tool to use so that you can begin training that brain of yours and releasing its chronic need to "freak out".

A great little practice that you can incorporate to get started is to meditate for just ten minutes, and then follow it by your favorite music. Studies show that incorporating even just ten minutes of meditation into your daily routine is optimal for supporting your brain in learning to relax. Giving it the time to learn how to tune out the outer world, and just experience peace, is crucial to your mental health. And the good news is that mediation is one of the easiest things you could ever do. All you do is sit down, close your eyes, clear your mind, and do nothing. This is where those synapses come into play again, creating new neural pathways that remind your brain that it is okay to calm down and relax every so often! Following it by good music is lovely, too.

Now, I wouldn't recommend following up your meditation session with Nirvana, Smells Like Teen Spirit or anything like that, but music has a way of "bringing you back to reality" from your meditation practice. It has a beautiful healing effect on our brains. Listening to some of your favorite music and getting up to move around afterwards can help to stimulate joy and positivity in your mind. If you love dancing, you can dance. If you don't fancy yourself as a dancer, just moving around and doing some chores around your house, or even working out, is great too. The idea is that you want to use the music as a tool to move the excess energy through you, so as to get back to feeling good again.

There are also many other personal rituals that you can create to support you in putting a pause on your "freak outs". Finding things that you love, and doing them whenever you need an extra relaxation-boost can help you greatly in letting go of your deep attachment to worry, and giving yourself the space that you need to actually enjoy life again. This can be anything from using your favorite bath products in the shower each morning, brewing your favorite coffee, or going to your favorite place that brings you peace. It can be different for different people. Take an inventory of the things that help to promote peace and relaxation within you, and make an effort to use those powerful tools to support you in retraining your brain to stop being so addicted to worry, and just chill the freak out.

EXERCISES

What do you usually worry about?

_____

_____

_____

_____

Recount an episode when your worries made you spiral into an anxiety attack

_____

_____

_____

_____

_____

What form of meditation can you do to practice staying in the moment?

_____

_____

_____

_____

What can you do to ensure you meditate consistently?

_____

_____

_____

_____

Write down the worst scenario that could happen if what you are worrying about comes true, whatever it is. Write it down.

_____

_____

_____

_____

Now, step back and take an inventory of just how true and realistic this worry is

_____

_____

_____

_____

_____

Has whatever you're worried about ever happened? If yes, how often? Were you able to deal with it? How did you do that?

_____

_____

_____

_____

What would you say to a friend of yours who confided in you about this worry? Write down your reasons not to worry, and what you would say to your worried friend.

_____

_____

_____

_____

CHAPTER 8
WORKING ON EMPTYING THE MIND

There are countless tools at our disposal to help us calm our thoughts and relax our minds. Deep breathing, meditation, music, and guided imagery are among the most effective.

Deep Breathing

Most of us take short, shallow breaths into our chests. This type of breathing can make you feel anxious. If you pay attention to your breathing, you may find that you're holding your breath at times, causing tightness in your chest.

The following deep breathing technique will teach how to take bigger breaths, deliver more oxygen to your body, expand your lung capacity, and release tension.

Get into a position that is comfortable for you. You can lie on the bed or floor using pillows to support your head and knees. You can also sit in a chair that supports your head, neck, and shoulders.

Slowly breathe in through your nose and allow your belly, so to say, to fill with air.

Slowly breathe out through your nose.

Gently place a hand on your chest and one on your stomach.

Your stomach should rise when you breathe in and lower as you breathe out. The hand on your stomach should move more than the one that's on your chest.

Continue breathing in this way for several minutes.

Deep Focus Breathing

Breath-Focus Breathing combines deep breathing with meditation:

Close your eyes; breathe in deeply just as you did in the deep breathing exercise.

Breathe in. Imagine that you're breathing in peace.

Breathe out. Imagine that you're exhaling stress.

Now use a word or phrase with your breath. As you breathe in, say it in your mind.

Repeat it as you breathe out.

Continue breathing in this way for several minutes.

Listen to Soothing Music

Music has been used for healing around the world for thousands of years. Aristotle considered music an appropriate therapy for certain conditions, and Plato recommended using it to treat anxiety.

Music has a massive effect on our mood. It can make us energetic, sad, joyous, or relaxed. Studies are now proving what the ancient Greeks already knew that music affects many biological processes, including blood pressure, respiration rates, and even reduces fatigue.

If you're feeling anxious or stressed, music may be one of the best ways to calm yourself. While everyone is different, these three types of music are relaxing. There's probably at least one type that will appeal to you. Sacred chants and mantras; Classical Music; Meditation music and natural sounds.

Meditate

Meditation is an influential tool for relaxing the mind. Not only do you reduce stress while you're meditating, but studies have also found that over time, the practice of meditation makes you more resistant to stress.

Consider meditating regularly to help you be less reactive to stress and reap the most benefit.

Mantra Meditation is an easy way to introduce the practice into your life.

Find a comfortable, quiet place. You'll eventually be able to meditate anywhere.

Choose your mantra. A mantra is merely a word or phrase which you repeat to yourself. It can be the traditional Hindu word, "Om," or you can use something meaningful to you, such as "Love" or "Peace."

Close your eyes and repeat your mantra to yourself while focusing on the mantra and nothing else. Don't worry if you find other thoughts entering your mind. Simply go back to your mantra.

You can start with 5 or 10 minute sessions until you work your way up to 20 or 30 minutes. If you do not have time for a longer session, you can break it into two shorter ones.

Use Guided Imagery

Guided Imagery is a suitable and simple relaxation technique that helps to eliminate stress in the body. It's a vivid daydream which you design yourself.

There are classes where a teacher guides you, and you can also use audio recordings. If you like, you can record your own or just use your inner voice and imagination.

How to Get Started:

Get comfortable by finding a position that will allow you to relax but not put you to sleep. You can utilize a comfortable chair or sit cross-legged on the floor.

Breathe from your diaphragm and close your eyes. Focus on breathing in and breathing out, releasing stress and inhaling peace. Let your belly expand and contract with your breath. Your shoulders shouldn't be rising and falling; if they are, you're not yet breathing in a relaxed way.

Once you're in a relaxed state, imagine yourself in the most beautiful and peaceful place. You might be floating in a cool, clear pool of water or sitting by a warm fire while wrapped in a cozy blanket. You may want to remember a place and time where you were relaxed, a scene from a movie or book, or a place you've always wanted to visit.

Involve all of your senses! What does it look like? How do you feel? What do you smell? Can you hear music, or a waterfall?

Stay in your happy dwelling for as long as you like. Enjoy the practice and allow yourself to be free of stress and problems.

Once you're ready to return, just count back from twenty and tell yourself that when you get to "one," you'll feel serene.

It may seem impossible to believe until you've done it, but when you return, you'll feel refreshed. It'll feel like you returned from a mini-vacation without leaving your room.

List any other methods you can think of that will help you to empty your mind

_____

_____

_____

_____

_____

CHAPTER 9

FEELING INFERIOR IN FAMILY, AT WORK, AND IN SOCIETY

Challenges Women Face in the Workplace

Despite having equal working and voting rights, women still face obvious gender bias in the workplace. In this 21st century, women struggle a lot in the tradeoff between family and work life. Often this means they have to sacrifice some success and status in the company, and in society. Sometimes they not only sacrifice their success, but also get less remuneration than their male counterparts. There are some common challenges which women face in the workplace, and among those are the following:

Pregnancy Discrimination:

At the time of having a baby, women face several complexities at the workplace. Although theoretically illegal, some of them may lose their position at the workplace, or even be fired. Many women are afraid of starting their family for the sake of their career. According to reports in The Guardian, almost 50,000 women were found to have become jobless as a result of pregnancy.

Sexual Harassment:

Nowadays, sexual harassment at work is still very common among women. At the workplace, superiors may try to lure the junior female employees by giving a salary-increase or promotion, only to start abusing them. Sometimes their colleagues are also involved. Not all male abusers are the same: some might force a girl, while some try to take advantage of a woman's friendliness.

The Gender Pay-Gap:

This is the bias when making remuneration to employees that means paying different salaries to different genders for the same rank. Some statistics have shown that women earn 24% less compared to men for the same rank. Women may be considered weaker or less capable than men, and the gap begins from there.

Race and Ethnicity:

At most workplaces, racial and ethnic discrimination exist. Although black women have been succeeding in their struggling for equality, they still face some challenges at the workplace. Black women may still receive less dignity and remuneration than other employees at the workplace. Adding to this, discrimination among and between women also exists. In some cases, for example, the "beautiful woman" gets more benefit from the boss and superiors compared to the "less beautiful woman".

Ego Clashes:

Personal egoism is another challenge for women in the workplace. Sometimes a man doesn't want to get orders from a woman who is superior to him. It's old-fashioned, but he thinks of her as being a threat. The ego of a man hinders him from seeing the professionalism or authority of a woman in a better position than him.

Climbing the Career Ladder:

Have you ever experienced that it's much harder for you as a woman to gain recognition and praise? We can see that in most of the corporations men occupy the main positions. You might find that women are not allowed to advance faster than men, despite having all the requisites for promotion. So, you need to be more focused on your professionalism, along with maintaining the wellbeing of your personality. There can be so many factors that hinder you from moving upward in your career. Sometimes it is right to speak out about an injustice; at other times what you need to do, is not to listen, and not to care about those hindrances. If you deserve such a position you will get it. So, move with confidence.

Appearance:

Women's appearance tends to be judged more strictly than men's appearance, and both sexes are judging. Women face criticism if they are not polished enough. On the other hand, if they pay too much attention to their appearance, others think they are trying to impress their superiors. Thus, it's very difficult for women in both cases, and confusion arises. A woman has to face the challenges in controlling both situations.

Work-Life Imbalance:

Another challenge that women face at the workplace is imbalance in their working life. Both their personal life and the working life suffer. Personal life suffers if they have to stay at work for a long time to finish some important tasks, for example. On the other hand, in their working life they face problems, as they may be stuck at home with some family situation. A woman has to maintain both the family as well as her professional life, and there are expectations on both sides.

Fear:

Fear is another great challenge for women at the workplace. Many women are scared about facing new challenges and they do not want to take risks. To overcome these fears, raise your voice and challenge the fear. Speak to yourself out loud. Maybe talk to other colleagues about how it is a challenge, but you are determined to face it. This will raise your confidence in facing that fear. Always remember: confidence is the best thing that works as the strength of a woman.

During that period of the Month...

every woman feels sick at that certain time, and it's no joke. It is a natural fact, and it's not under the control of women. In this time, you will find it harder to work well compared to other days, and it's very challenging for you. Be patient, and use your experience to be understanding of the colleague who has headaches. To understand your fellow female co-workers, because they, too, have to deal with this... and realize that there's an upside. When you're out of this, you'll have days of happier moods. Be as vivacious then as you feel, and grateful for feeling stronger and more positive.

EXERCISES

What struggles do you face in the workplace? Describe them below

_____

_____

_____

_____

What is it about your job that makes you happiest?

_____

_____

_____

_____

What are your strengths in the workplace? Are you putting those strengths to good use?

_____

_____

_____

_____

What are you most proud of professionally? Why?

_____

_____

_____

Does your job leave you feeling professionally fulfilled? Does it make you happy ? Why or why not ?

_____

_____

_____

What are you grateful for at work ?

_____

_____

_____

What do you like or dislike about the company culture ?

_____

_____

_____

Dependency

The term "dependency" refers to someone being controlled by others. It is a type of relationship where you depend on others in making decisions regarding education, income, working, taking steps regarding new things, etc. Dependency ruins the inner courage to do something on your own, which in turn destroys your self-confidence. Dependency also means handling the balance between conditions, tasks, and events, so that you might find yourself unable to move forward or plan until some previous step is completed.

A dependent person wants to do everything with the permission of the one who dominates them. The dependent person can even get to the stage of being like a slave, and have to act according to the person on whom he or she is dependent. The result will be that the dependent person has no self-esteem.

The opposite term of dependency is "self-dependency", which signifies having a high level of self-esteem, self-confidence, self-assurance and self-empowerment. A self-dependent person can obey someone when it's called for, but she doesn't have to get approval in order to go ahead with anything. She has an ability to make her own decisions, and she can trust her own conclusions. This isn't refusal to collaborate: such a woman is taking responsibility for what she learns from others. Self-dependency is the foundation for attaining self-esteem, self-love and empowerment; it inspires a woman to explore the world and to aspire to improving her circumstances.

We used to see that women were dependent on men in most workplaces. They were not able to make any decision, even in the basics. They were dominated by men at home, and often not allowed to go out to find work. Now situations have changed, and as a woman you have many more opportunities to be self-dependent.

You can make your own decisions, you can work outside the home, raise your voice for your rights; and men do not have to dominate you. If self-dependency is very important for women to gain self-esteem, then how can women can gain or increase their self-esteem through self-dependency? You will advance by means of the following ways:

Standing Alone:

To become self-confident, you have to stand alone, because no relationships stay forever, not even the parent-child relationship. Strong relationships can sometimes, unfortunately, make us dependent on others and make us obey them like servants. Self-confidence is said to occur whenever you stand your position at the time of having the disapproval of others. Each time you withstand the test of the relationship, you become less scared of being separated from everyone else, or being alone. When you take this detachment as a positive sign, you become independent. Thus, self-esteem comes in the form of standing alone.

Self-Knowledge:

Self-knowledge or "know thyself" is a term which means to understand your inner mind, emotions and reason, to be able to analyze and motivate yourself. Human behavior is full of complexity in thinking and feeling. Self-knowledge is also about knowing your emotions, as human emotions are continuously changing. Women are capable of control of their emotions. Self-dependency makes you differentiate between emotional judgements. Women must have clear knowledge about what emotions they should accept feeling in a given situation, and what they should work to overcome. No-one but you can know your reality and manufacture your convictions. Understanding your own emotion makes you independent and empowers your freedom, which then leads to having higher self-esteem.

Increased Confidence:

Confidence comes from knowledge and achievement. This achievement is about conquering your fear of separation. Your ability to become independent grows as you stand up for yourself. This isn't something you get in one day, but rather a skill you learn over time. Confidence comes naturally from perseverance. A self-independent woman has the confidence to work alone and make the necessary decisions on her own. Thus, self-confident women are enabled to have high self-esteem.

Strong, Independent Relationships:

Confident people construct solid bonds with others. In those sorts of connections, every individual shares their emotions and feelings straightforwardly. They meet up to share common qualities and legitimate feelings. They join through shared goals and associate through qualities. These strong relationships have an implication in enhancing the kind of self-dependency which will lead women as they seek to build higher self-esteem.

Leadership:

Self-dependent women have the ability to lead others. Leaders are at the top and enjoy being in the position alone; they have a vision, and persuade others to embrace or fulfill the same. Self-confidence comes from knowledge and self-dependency. Leaders are independent in their decisions and can consult other players in the group they lead, but do not depend on others to make them. Women leaders can be independent enough to lead them to secure, high self-esteem.

Question: How would you describe your dependency level? If you are highly dependent, why do you think that is ?

_____

_____

_____

_____

_____

Overcome the Challenges

Women face many challenges at the workplace, and they face more challenges compared to men. In spite of this, they can overcome those obstacles in different ways. Here are some means by which women can bypass or overcome these challenges:

Learn How to Enhance the Opportunities in Your Career:

One of the major challenges of women is lack of opportunity. To overcome this, why not step forward to the organization's manager to ask for some training sessions that will improve your skills, and get the opportunity being offered to you? It's your responsibility to grab this or any other opportunity, whenever it comes to you.

Recognize Yourself as an Expert:

Nowadays every organization seeks expert people in a specific area. Suppose you have proficiency in a specific topic, and the manager of the organization perceives you as being an expert. In that case, opportunities will come for you as your manager has the idea that you have the expertise for this specific task. Put your special skills and experience on your CV/resumé where they can be seen easily. Don't be ashamed to show what you can do, or what you know about. You may be pleasantly surprised when your boss praises you by giving remuneration or a pay-rise. Thus, become an expert at a specific task.

Figure out How to Make Yourself More Interesting to Hiring Managers:

In these days of marketing, make yourself a most marketable product. To do this, you have to increase your knowledge and skill required for the job you want. Ensure that you have unique skills that no one else has. This could mean doing your own studies outside of work, going on a course or conference in your own time, or reading about interesting, relevant subjects. If they want volunteers, then you volunteer! You have to grab the attention of the hiring manager, and you will do so when you can show that you have the skills or experience that no one else has.

Be Bold:

You always have to be bold. That means you have to be at the forefront in your career, and have to be prepared to get the opportunities coming your way. If the situation does not turn out as you expected, you have to be prepared to take the risks and handle the disappointment or drawbacks. If you have failed in several stages, you should learn from the experiences. Boldness isn't being evasive when you admit your mistakes. Admit them boldly, without shame; and use the experience in your career for facing some future challenge.

Learn How to Negotiate:

Negotiation skills are important to everyone, especially for a woman, as they help her to grab the opportunity, to get the right and to raise her voice for herself. It enables women to secure the job, wage or salary, promotions, increments, etc. As a result, to overcome the challenges that you face at the workplace, you have to learn strong negotiating skills.

Describe a life-changing event you experienced

_____

_____

_____

_____

Write down how you plan to overcome your limiting beliefs

_____

_____

_____

_____

_____

List 3 ways you intend to get out of your comfort zone

List 3 quotes that motivate you to achieve more goals in your life

CHAPTER 10

MAKING BETTER LIFE DECISIONS

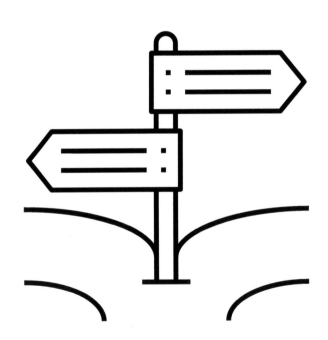

Living with A Purpose

Being purposeful is about being sure of what you want and having a plan that helps you to achieve it. Deep inspirational goals and aspirations always go together with a plan.

Asking yourself the "What can I do?" question in various situations and areas of your life allows you to challenge your mind to develop solutions and plans that bring forth the actualization of aims, goals, and dreams. For instance, if you want a great relationship, "What can you do..." to ensure that your aim becomes your daily life?

This question makes you more purposeful about your pursuit, because it is focused, it's specific. It places you in this day, it makes you think of smaller, practical steps to a goal; and when you are purposeful, you are more assured and confident.

You are the only person capable of deciding what you want, and therefore what you have to do to achieve it, and what it means to you. Take responsibility for yourself and your life by taking responsibility for your daily time and life.

The more responsible you are with your time, resources, attention, intention, and effort, the likelier you are to be more successful, confident, and purposeful in living your life. You are also likely to be happier with yourself and with where you are in your life. Put yourself on the path to daily personal development in all major areas of your life!

I am aware that you probably have many goals and aspirations, so, you have to be responsible with how you use your time and resources. Instead of multi-tasking or pursuing many goals simultaneously, which is likely to overwhelm you, cause low motivation and low self-confidence, pursue one goal at a time, solve one problem at a time, and handle one thing at a time in all areas of your life, every single day of your life. It's hard at first: you literally have to put the other things on a mental shelf for a day, an hour, or whatever.

By narrowing your intention and attention, i.e., what you want and what you have to do to achieve it, which requires time, you become surer of the effort you must take to achieve your primary aim. This clarity allows you to be purposeful with your daily habits, time, effort, and overall wellbeing while you pursue your goals, aims, dreams and aspirations.

Many of us know the changes we need to implement to make our lives better, but often fail to do so, instead opting to maintain the status quo. To become more purposeful and therefore more confident and self-assured, adopt the "now mentality", the mentality that allows you to stop postponing yourself, your goals, your aspirations, and stop neglecting the very thing your psyche truly craves.

Whenever you set an intention, and you decide to do or improve something, also make immediate changes or take immediate action - the "now mentality" - so that you can create the momentum you need to achieve a critical mass and success in key pillars of your life.

Becoming purposeful with your life is possible when you adopt what you want to achieve as a fundamental part of your daily life. Adopting the habit of purposeful practice allows you to become intentional with regard to your daily pursuits and the results of these pursuits on your overall wellbeing, peace of mind, success, and confidence. Whether you are working on a spiritual, physical, or mental aspect of your life, make its practice an integral component of your daily life. Consistent practice is the difference between self-actualization, and a life full of discontentment and unfulfilled potential.

Your vision is a representation of what you would like to achieve within specific areas of your life. When you have a clear vision of the achievements you would like to have under your belt, or the kind of person you would like to be one, five, or ten years from now, it gives you the clarity you need to be purposeful with how you use all your resources, including intention, attention, time, energy and effort.

Creating a vision board, a sort of master-timeline that shows what you intend to achieve and the kind of individual you want to become, will prove to be very useful to you here.
At the start of each endeavor or aim, set an intention, a desired outcome. For example, at the beginning of the day, set the intention to be more mindful and purposeful with your decisions and actions.
Attaching intentions to all your decisions, aims, endeavors, and daily undertakings allows you to reconnect with the present moment, who you are or want to become, and determine whether the intention and attention given to the activity at hand are congruent with your desires or aims.

By choosing how you want to be, feel, or act, you become more purposeful, at peace and content, and more successful and confident in key areas of your life.
Having a grand purpose or vision for your life is great. Still, to achieve anything substantial and to move forward with poise and confidence, you also need to think small and infuse simplicity into your grand scheme... because only by doing so can you curtail your natural tendency to overestimate what you can achieve within a given period.
Yes, having a grand dream is great; but break it down into simpler steps that build up to it and make it easier to achieve your chief aim.

When you are purposeful, you avoid feeling overwhelmed and instead become surer of your decisions and actions, knowing that their undertaking helps you to create the life you want to live and experience.

Practical Advice

Listen to Your Inner Voice

Remember, only you know who you are. So, make the world see you that way. Do not be swayed by what others tell you. You have to have faith that you are worthy. The world ought to respect you. You have been through a lot, and whenever things are going wrong, it seems as if they will never get better. You may be at the worst juncture of your life. If so, it's good that you are there, because it cannot become any worse now. It will only begin to get better from here on! You have been through adversities before. Each time you did, you came out a stronger person. And you will, once again.

Investigate Your Source of Low Self-Esteem

Before you pull yourself up from this abyss of low self-worth, you need to find the cause of your sentiments. What happened that made you feel this way? Was it truly something you did? The answer to this could be 'yes'. It's not always another person's fault: sometimes it is us. If so, accept it and move on. We all make mistakes. If we didn't, 80% of this city's service providers like divorce lawyers, psychiatrists, and counselors would be out of jobs. You are making mistakes, and that's normal. So, don't dwell on the past. Look forward to how you can mend your mistakes.

Evaluate Your Self-Esteem

Yes, you heard right. Evaluate your self-esteem. Measure it. You cannot do it on the bathroom scale or the kitchen scale. The question you're asking yourself is, "What scale do I use?" Well, you are the scale. This will take some time. You will have to reflect and determine the weight. Given a measure of one to ten, where would you place yourself? How would you rate your self-esteem? If it is lower than you want, where would you want it to be?

Self-Exploration

You need to make good use of yourself as a person, and this means you have to know exactly who you are. You must have every single idea about your personality, your mental state, your emotional state, your feelings and thoughts towards every single situation, your likes and dislikes, and the kind of people you want to spend your life with. This permits you to take full control of yourself and explore your inner world without facing any difficulties or challenges.

EXERCISES

Write down four goals you can achieve that will help bring you closer to your purpose:

What do your inner voice and self-esteem say about you ?

How can you change your inner voice and self-esteem to be more encouraging and confident?

_____

_____

_____

_____

_____

_____

Imagine your life after you made an important choice. Visualize your life 3 years from now – what does it look like?

_____

_____

_____

_____

_____

_____

What is the worst scenario if you make the choice you want? What can you do to limit the downside?

_____

_____

_____

_____

_____

_____

What is the best decision you ever made ? Why ?

_____

_____

_____

_____

_____

_____

Did you ever regret not making a decision in your life? Why?

_____

_____

_____

_____

_____

_____

When you had the opportunity, did you choose courage over comfort?

_____

_____

_____

_____

_____

_____

Why are you doing what you are doing?

_____

_____

_____

_____

_____

Write down some of your decisions that made you who you are today

_____

_____

_____

_____

_____

CHAPTER 11

CHANGING THE MINDSET

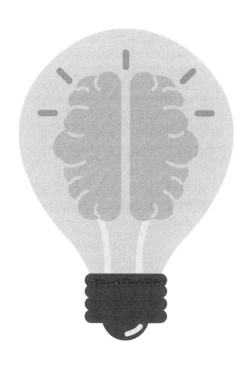

Another useful cognitive tool is establishing new core beliefs. This strategy focuses not only on the thoughts that are negatively contributing to your daily life, but also on the core beliefs you are reinforcing through inaccurate thinking patterns. Think of the core beliefs as your personal rule book.

For example, Sarah learned to reframe her negative thoughts to help her to decrease anxiety and increase self-esteem. Here, she takes this practice a step further and identifies the thinking habits that led to those negative core beliefs that were inhibiting her confidence and happiness.

Sarah, like many women who grow up with the titles of responsible, mature, and good girl, developed a way of thinking that led her to believe she was either all good or all bad, all the time. When she made mistakes, she saw them as huge disasters and dwelled on them for weeks, which sharply curbed her motivation to try new things, or step outside her comfort zone. She had strong reactions to her manager's and colleagues' suggestions and ideas because she believed that in order to be smart and capable, she had to be right all the time. She responded negatively to critique or criticism, believing it overwhelmed all her positive progress. Over time, Sarah became uncomfortable "putting herself out there", whether on training courses, at work, or in social situations.

Negative Core Beliefs

There are numerous cognitive distortions, or inaccurate ways of thinking, that reinforce negative emotions and thoughts. These distortions feel true, but they are actually the result of your brain's effort to make connections, even when connections do not exist or are incorrect. The resulting inaccurate thoughts shore up your bad feelings about yourself and your judgments of others.

Low self-confidence can usually be tied to one (or more) of these inaccurate thinking patterns. These patterns also have the tendency to feed off each other, and it is common to have multiple thought patterns that lead to the same negative core belief.

The most common cognitive distortions are outlined here. You will see Sarah's negative core beliefs reflected in several of them. How many do you recognize in your own thought patterns?

All-or-Nothing Thinking

Also known as black-and-white thinking, this cognitive distortion is characterized by the belief that all people, things, and events are inherently good or bad, wrong or right, true or false, with no possibility of middle ground or shades of gray. You're either all in or all out. There is no in-between. The worry with this type of thinking is that mistakes are thought of as being proof of poor character or incompetence, rather than learning experiences. Another dangerous aspect of this type of thinking is that you look at other people through the same distorted view, which can lead to unfair judgment and lack of tolerance.

When Sarah thinks that making straight A's is the only option for future success, she is telling herself that anything less than an A makes her unsuccessful. She has set herself up for decreased confidence if she is unable to get an A. When she makes mistakes and believes this is indicative of her incompetence, this is another example of how all-or-nothing thinking patterns can lead to limiting core beliefs. You can see how this can then spill over into Sarah's personal life and relationships

"Should" and "Must"

'Should' and 'must' are ways of thinking that follow specific rules. Sarah thinks she should be a good daughter and sister, she must visit her family frequently, and she should take care of them. Putting this pressure on herself leads to resentment, as she recognized when she was working to identify the root of her negative thinking patterns. Now she can see which thought processes contributed to the development of these rules.

This cognitive distortion can be tied to all the "shoulds and musts" women learn as young girls. Some are self-taught, as women often put unreasonable expectations on themselves. No matter what their origin is, these distorted ways of thinking can lead to decreased self-confidence and self-esteem, when it becomes impossible to play by your own rule book!

Jumping to Conclusions

When we jump to conclusions, we make assumptions about someone else's motivations, future actions, or thoughts. When Sarah's friend Ann canceled plans at the last minute because she wasn't feeling well, Sarah immediately assumed Ann no longer wanted to be her friend, but it is far more likely that Ann canceled because she had a headache. Her action has nothing to do with Sarah, but Sarah's inaccurate thoughts lead her to that conclusion. This thought that results from the cognitive distortion can become a negative core belief: I am not likable. People do not want to be my friend.

Personalization

Not everything is about you. Most people are making decisions based on what is best for themselves, their families, and their work. Allowing your thoughts to make this personal does not serve you and only increases unhappiness.

When Sarah receives corrective criticism from her manager about a work project, she thinks, I knew he didn't like me. He's so critical of everything I do. She is using personalization. Rather than assuming her manager cares about the outcome and wants her to succeed, she is allowing distorted thinking to make a connection that does not exist. Her manager's feelings toward her may have nothing to do with his critique, but her thinking process causes her to make this erroneous connection. This leads to a negative viewpoint of not only herself but also her manager, and her experience in the workplace suffers as a result.

Negative Predictions

Also known as catastrophizing, this type of thinking leads to focusing on one negative aspect and maximizing it to great importance. Sarah's tendency toward all-or-nothing thinking goes well with this cognitive distortion because she frequently turns one negative—usually a critique or a mistake - into a prediction of a future failure.

Sarah decided to go on a blind date with a woman who never called her afterward. Sarah catastrophized this event, thinking, I will never find my soulmate. She allowed her thoughts to maximize one incident to gigantic proportions and make an erroneous prediction about the future.

If Sarah was not using this distorted thinking process, she may have thought that although this woman was not a good match, the right person and relationship was out there. This would lead to more confidence, and Sarah would be more open to future opportunities to meet other people, which would increase the likelihood of this belief becoming reality.

Filtering

Another negative type of thinking occurs when you filter out positive details in favor of negative ones. Sarah's thoughts frequently follow this pattern. She focuses on her perceived failures while completely discounting all the things she does well. This is especially apparent in her assessment of her physical attributes and abilities at work. Sarah focuses on the negatives (My nose is too big, I need to lose weight) instead of using positive self-talk (My eyes are my best physical feature, I have a beautiful smile). Her negative thinking patterns literally filter out and disregard the positives.

Overgeneralizing

Using one incident, statement, or moment to make assumptions about yourself or someone else is known as overgeneralizing. When Sarah makes one mistake at work and immediately thinks "", she is overgeneralizing her abilities in a negative way. Sarah does things right most of the time, but her inaccurate thought process leads her to use this event to make the wrong assumption, which also contributes to negative self-talk and her decreased self-confidence.

She interprets her manager's comments as being overly critical, which turns into a core-belief that he is always critical. Overgeneralizing turns into rules about yourself and others, which can become negative core-beliefs.

Blaming

Just as you are not responsible for the happiness of others, others are not responsible for your happiness. Blaming is when you hold others accountable for your feelings, actions, or consequences. If you notice this kind of thinking (She made me feel so guilty; It's his fault I made this mistake; She made me feel stupid in that meeting), you are using this thought process. Blaming takes away your power to control your thoughts and emotions, and places it on others. This leads to core-beliefs that you are not in control of your emotions, or that others have all the power, which decreases your self-confidence.

Reasoning Based on Emotion

Emotions are powerful, but they do not always reflect the truth.

When Sarah feels an overwhelming sense of responsibility for her parents and siblings, does that mean that she is truly responsible for them? Of course not. But because she feels it so acutely, this distortion leads her to believe it is the truth, which then influences her core beliefs and subsequent decisions.

Fantasy of Control.

So much of our behavior, thoughts, and actions come from the idea that control is good and keeps us safe. When you worry about the future, it does not prevent bad things from happening, insulate you from future pain, or prepare you to handle the worst. The fantasy of control is the inaccurate belief that we have absolute control over everything. When things do not work out as you intended, your confidence decreases—which is unfortunate, because it wasn't likely that it was under your control in the first place. If you find yourself becoming extremely frustrated when you are stuck in traffic, pay attention to the negative beliefs swirling in your mind, such as, I should have known not to go this way. This kind of thinking indicates that a fantasy of control is distorting your thought process by suggesting you could have predicted or controlled this outcome.
Practice control over your emotions, behavior, and reactions. Recognize when your thoughts are being distorted by the inaccurate idea that you have control over the weather, traffic, or other people's emotions, behaviors, and reactions.

What types of cognitive distortions, i.e. unreasonable thoughts, do you most often suffer? Write down a few examples.

_____

_____

_____

_____

_____

Chain of Questions

When faced with a negative thought or fear of a negative outcome, ask yourself, "What then?" Follow each response with "What then?" until you get to the root cause or bigger implication of why a negative outcome is frightening you. Identifying the worst-case scenario and recognizing that it is not that scary can help you let go of the fear of a negative outcome. If you look at the worst possible outcome and acknowledge you could handle it, even if it's not ideal, you have taken away the power of the unknown.

Try it! Write down a negative thought or fear and answer the chain of questions below. ✍

Negative thought or fear:

_____

What then?

_____

What then?

_____

What then?

_____

Identifying Patterns

Think about your own negative core beliefs. Can you identify which cognitive distortions led you to those beliefs? Notice if any patterns arise. Many distortions in thinking go hand in hand, such as overgeneralizing and jumping to conclusions, blaming and personalization, filtering, and all-or-nothing thinking.

Establishing New Core-Beliefs

Once you are aware of the cognitive distortions that are driving your thought processes, you can more easily recognize when you are using them to make inaccurate connections. Developing this skill takes time and patience. Much like your automatic negative thoughts, negative core beliefs about yourself and your world can have a great effect on your confidence and self-esteem. These core beliefs take the negative thoughts to a deeper level, where they become ingrained ways of making connections. The core beliefs become your personal rule-book in influencing how you live, act, and relate to others. Establishing new core-beliefs is exciting new territory. Visualize this process as throwing out the old maps, and establishing your own paths to happiness and confidence.

Understand Past Events

Although you do not want to dwell in the past, evaluating previous events can be helpful in understanding why certain thoughts and beliefs have taken hold. You learned your negative beliefs from other people, as a result of experiences or as a method of self-preservation or protection from feelings that may have seemed dangerous or overwhelming.

Everyone uses these inaccurate thought processes occasionally because our brains have a negative bias, which means it's easier to focus on negative events and make negative connections when trying to make sense of the world. But with practice, we can make those connections more positive and automatic. One way to practice these positive switches is to focus on the good side of a negative core-belief.

Focus on the Good

A useful process in changing negative beliefs is flipping them around to a positive statement, and then looking for evidence that the positive statement is correct. For example, when the negative belief *I'm not good enough for that new position* is flipped into a positive statement, it becomes *I am good enough for that new position*. Focus on the evidence to support this: *I work hard; I always try my best, I am loyal to the company; my customers can depend on me.*

Another common negative belief I hear in my practice is *I'm not a good enough mother*. In the session, I flip this into the positive statement *I am a good enough mother*, and then ask the client to provide evidence that this is true. Eventually, she will come up with statements such as *I feed my children; I keep them safe; I take care of them when they are sick; I tell them I love them*. This leads her to discover more and more evidence that the statement is true, which challenges the negative core belief.

Try any of these strategies to keep you in a positive mindset:

- Make a visual reminder of positive beliefs you are working to uphold. Use a combination of uplifting phrases and quotes to keep you in this mindset. Find phrases and quotes online that resonate with you, take screenshots, and keep them in a folder on your phone. Print them and use them to beautify your walls, write them directly on sticky notes, or use them to start a vision board.
- Try to spend more time with individuals who are also working on maintaining positivity and confidence in themselves. Confidence is contagious.
- Recognize these cognitive distortions in others around you. Give them grace and patience, as they may not have the same understanding you recently gained but do limit your exposure to their negativity and distorted beliefs.
- As always, practice self-care and compassion. This work takes time, but it is worth it.

How can you be more intentional today?

_____

_____

_____

_____

_____

_____

What lies is your inner critic telling you? How are these holding you back?

_____

_____

_____

_____

What change are you resisting? In what ways can you grow to adapt to this change?

_____

_____

_____

_____

How are your emotions limiting your mindset?

_____

_____

_____

_____

Write down some episodes that boosted your mindset ✍

_____

_____

_____

_____

_____

How is your physical health affecting your mindset? How can you fix this? ✍

_____

_____

_____

_____

_____

How do you react to negative situations? Write down how you feel ✍

_____

_____

_____

_____

_____

CHAPTER 12

WHY DO WOMEN EXPERIENCE BODY SHAMING?

Self-esteem is fundamental to identity and a critical ingredient in anyone's ability to feel genuine happiness. It helps us to feel validated from within, but sometimes, despite having a strong resolve, this self-worth can be toppled by external forces. Women are especially susceptible to this as the media and society at large control what is "acceptable," particularly in terms of appearance, behavior, and societal roles.

The Body Question for Women

Body image is all about how we see our physical selves. A distorted body image is an unrealistic perception of one's own body. The official term is 'body dysmorphia', and we all have it to some degree. For most women, it's a simple and easy thing to manage with a little rationality and common sense. Growing more comfortable in your own skin also comes with maturity.

Much like overall self-esteem in general, negative body image can stem from childhood experiences, as well as an unhealthy comparison with the rest of society later in life. Of course, friends and family also play a role here. Even though you may fall within the normal weight range, a distorted body image can result from statements like, "If you just lose those last 5 pounds, you'd look really great". These seemingly well-intentioned and subtle suggestions can have a big impact over time if you do not learn to manage your thoughts properly.

Not ever feeling attractive enough is an exhausting emotion to harbor. The question, therefore, may be: "Is there a way to stop being too critical of your physical appearance? Will there be a time when you won't obsess about the tiniest of flaws?" Again, this comes partly with age, but if you wish to combat this in a more proactive manner, the following are the warning signs of negative or distorted body image to watch out for:

• Being overly observant of your features when looking in mirrors,
• Obsessively comparing yourself to others,
• Being constantly envious of role models and celebrities.

Just like problems with low self-esteem, a negative body image isn't something to be solved by sweeping it under the rug. In order for proper recovery to take place, it's important to recognize the problem, to begin with; to acknowledge the negative feelings that you are currently dealing with. To discover how to make your body feel comfortable, whilst eradicating the irrational thoughts of not being enough.

Movement and dance therapy are great alternative methods to improve one's body image. They can be used as a tool to help you to build trust and appreciate your body through creative expression and experimentation. It will feel strange and uncomfortable at first, but I have seen many women flower once just a small degree of competence is achieved. It's a liberating practice with so many confidence-building and health-related benefits.

Connection with Your Body

We are all different, and should be encouraged to embrace these differences. Oftentimes we can't help but aspire to these ideals, to have that perfect physique or face, to resemble that actress or TV presenter...

We know intuitively that it's really what's on the inside that matters. Our physical bodies shouldn't have to be a determining factor of our worth, nor should it overbearingly affect the way we feel about ourselves. However, this is a difficult concept to grasp for most, especially those who already have a poor self-image. More often than not, they are already dealing with feelings of self-hate and worthlessness, and they may well be on their way to triggering depression, or developing an eating disorder, in extreme cases.

In this sense, a negative self-image is going to have a huge impact on relationships, no matter what kind. It will affect how we feel and how we interact with others on every level. This almost always puts undue pressure on couples. In a romantic relationship, the partner of someone who has a negative self-image will usually offer words of encouragement to counter the negativity, hoping to solve the problem. Unfortunately, even the most well-intentioned words and honest compliments will fall on deaf ears to those with a poor self-image. This will spark additional tensions and inevitably cause the relationship to suffer.

It can also affect a couple's intimacy. Someone who doesn't feel satisfied about the way they look, will typically struggle with intimacy. Feelings of unattractiveness and low self-confidence will cause them to second-guess their partner's feelings and attraction towards them. They may feel uncomfortable being touched or being naked in front of them.

If you feel that you're dealing with poor self-image, and you notice that it's already affecting your relationships and life in general, you should consider having a self-image makeover. Here are some of the things you can do to achieve this, albeit slowly:

Choose to see your accomplishments

Dwelling on your outer appearance all the time isn't going to do you any good. You don't look like anybody else, and if you keep on comparing yourself to those around you, there will always be instances when you are going to fall short. Instead of nitpicking all your physical flaws, channel your energy into reminding yourself of what you're good at.

Say "No" to negative self-talk

Women can be extremely critical of themselves; somehow, it's easy for us to see our flaws when we look in the mirror. Whilst we already know that no-one is perfect and that there will always be details we wish we could change about ourselves, the ability to accept oneself wholly is what truly sets happy people apart from those who have a negative self-image.

This isn't going to be an overnight change, of course. The transition from negative to positive thinking can take some time, so you have to be patient with yourself. Keep those negative thoughts at bay, and do a little more each day to start that snowball of positive self-image rolling, bit-by-bit.

Take "baby steps"

If you are really dissatisfied with your physical appearance to the point that even shifting your thoughts isn't working, your list of viable solutions for achieving happiness will become shorter. You can try harder and be more enduring when fully accepting yourself, or you can do something to change what you dislike about your body by focusing on one small change at a time.

Instead of signing up for the gym, dance class, and new diet plan all in one go, knock each one off a month at a time. Start with just 30 minutes of exercise per day for the first month, walking, cycling or swimming, etc. Then add in that Pilates class once a week the following month. Once you have these activities fully rocking, start improving your diet with cleaner carbohydrates and reduced sugar meals. Taking on these tasks one at a time makes them exponentially easier to achieve, and more critically sustainable in the long term.

Open yourself up to others

This will be the most difficult for some, but if you want to stop viewing yourself in such a negative light, you need to start letting the people around you know how you truly feel. This is required all the more if you are in a committed relationship. Your significant other shouldn't be kept in the dark about the anxieties you feel regarding your self-image. You need to open up to them, and in doing so, they'll understand more about what you're going through, as well as the reasons for your actions and behaviors. The more they know, the more they'll be able to figure out a way to help you with getting through your troubles.

Sometimes, even the support of loved ones may fall short in talking you out of your negative self-image. In such instances, it might be best to talk to a counselor about your feelings. A professional's opinions can help you to gain a better perspective of your situation, and they can explain to you how to manage your negative thoughts. They will be able to help you to understand what triggers your poor self-image, and lead you to solutions that can greatly improve how you see yourself.

These seemingly small steps can be the change you need in order to make a big difference in getting your happiness back on track. The key is to integrate small changes into your life little by little, in ways that are not overwhelming but will definitely help you to gain a healthier disposition each day. Regaining a healthier self-image is a marathon, not a sprint. Making just a 1% improvement each week will compound into a huge improvement in no time at all.

Your Body as a Teacher

There's no getting away from it; popular consensus highly regards "thinness" as a factor of beauty in this day and age. Whilst this perception may be changing somewhat in recent years, I would still argue that this notion holds true in the minds of most women. It's often portrayed to go hand-in-hand with success, wealth, and social status. We see images of slender women in almost every form of media, magazines, on television, billboards, movies, and so on. Due to this constant bombardment, many women are driven to believe that achieving this level of appearance is the answer to getting everything they wish from life.

The subconscious mind reverts to the habit of comparing yourself to others in this regard. Friends, family, and significant others also play their part. These people may frequently and explicitly tell you less-than-favorable things about the way you look. It can be difficult to ignore these individuals entirely. Your close and constant proximity to them, in addition to valuing their opinions by default, makes it easy to spiral down into negative thinking, if you are not careful.

Another culprit worth mentioning is the highly influential and profitable weight-loss industry. Whilst some of these companies do have our best interests at heart, especially the more nutritionally based and health-centric businesses, others simply exist to sell us false dreams of a better life by counting calories, or worse, crash-dieting. They thrive on our insecurities, which ultimately results in us purchasing their products and trying their fad diets, in order to achieve our dreams for the small fee of $49!

They are banking on the belief that we are not enough, that they are on hand to help, that their weight-loss products and programs can make us feel happy and complete once more. Whilst it's a good idea to exercise regularly and eat clean foods to maintain a healthy weight, it should be done primarily for the sake of better health, and not to seek validation from others.

Valuing Your Body

Most lowly individuals do not have a confidence problem. They have an insecurity problem.

They don't trust themselves enough that they will make the right decisions. They have some physical insecurity - it's fearing that either they're too fat, too thin, too short, or too tall. They never run out of excuses because they keep on failing.

They don't believe in what they can do. They don't believe in their own worth.

This is obviously not a good thing. How do you expect other people to look at you as if you're valuable, if you yourself don't see it that way?

As Jordan Peterson said, "Treat yourself as someone responsible for helping."

You have to realize your own value before other people can.

Action Guide

Know what you can bring to the table. Are you a good negotiator? Are you a good passer? Are you a good songwriter? Are you a good teacher?

Whatever your skills are, nurture them and show them to the world. We all have something to donate to this world. It doesn't matter what it is. For some, it'll be solving the water crisis; for some, it'll be as simple as being a mango farmer. One doesn't have to be "bigger" than the other. We're all unique with our own set of gifts. Our job is to use that gift in the best way possible.

Value your body before anyone else does.

How do you react to negative situations? Write down how you feel

_____

_____

_____

_____

_____

Valuing Your Body

Most lowly individuals do not have a confidence problem. They have an insecurity problem.

They don't trust themselves enough that they will make the right decisions. They have some physical insecurity - it's either they're too fat, too thin, too short, or too tall. They never run out of excuses because they keep on failing.

They don't believe in what they can do. They don't believe in their own worth.

This is obviously not a good thing. How do you expect other people to look at you as if you're valuable if you yourself don't see it that way?

As Jordan Peterson said, "treat yourself as someone responsible for helping."

You have to realize your own value before other people can.

Action Guide

Know what you can bring to the table. Are you a good negotiator? Are you a good passer? Are you a good songwriter? Are you a good teacher?

Whatever your skills are, nurture them and show them to the world. We all have something to donate to this world. It doesn't matter what it is. For some, it'll be solving the water crisis; for some, it'll be as simple as being a mango farmer. One doesn't have to be "bigger" than the other. We're all unique with our own set of gifts. Our job is to use that gift in the best way possible.

Value your body before anyone else does.

Write down the criticism you usually give yourself regarding your body. Next to each, reframe the sentence and make it more loving and positive

_____

_____

_____

_____

_____

_____

How has your body image impacted your daily life?

_____

_____

_____

_____

_____

What have been your satisfactions and triumphs with your body image over time?

_____

_____

_____

_____

_____

Write about what you have denied and allowed yourself because of your perception of your body.

_____

_____

_____

_____

_____

_____

How has your self-esteem changed because of your sense of your appearance?

_____

_____

_____

_____

_____

_____

Write down a list of what you'd like to do when you will be confident with your body. For example: Find your love, find your dream job, have a better sex life, etc.

_____

_____

_____

_____

_____

Now re-read the list and ask yourself what is stopping you from doing these things now

_____

_____

_____

_____

_____

Sometimes we focus so much on how our bodies LOOK, that we forget to be grateful for everything our bodies can DO.

These are just some of the things that your body can do: Walking, engaging in sports, receiving a massage, having sex, keeping you alive!

Make a list of what your body can accomplish.

_____

_____

_____

_____

_____

What are you most grateful for?

_____

_____

_____

_____

_____

Write an encouraging letter to your body

CHAPTER 13

CARING FOR YOUR INTELLECTUAL NEEDS

Your Intellectual Needs

The brain is one of the most underrated parts of the body. It's always working, even when we are unaware that it's at work. Our brain helps us judge and evaluate situations, make plans, solve complex problems, and remember the past. Though it's such a small part of our body (only about three pounds!) it has a massive responsibility. Because the brain operates so effortlessly, it can be easy to forget just how vulnerable it is throughout our lives to diminished performance. We all know that physical exercise and movement are necessary for the body to stay strong and healthy. Well, the same is correct for our brains.

To help your brain to function to the best of its ability for as long as possible, you need to exercise it. Intellectual self-care is an exercise for your brain; it's doing things that keep your brain sharp. It is a lifelong commitment to learning new things that include opening yourself up to unfamiliar experiences, exercising your creativity, and challenging your brain to solve problems and embrace knowledge. When you exercise your brain, it helps you to function better across the board. I've seen intellectual self-care work wonders in my own life, as well as in the lives of my clients.

You might be thinking, "I'm okay with learning new things, but I'm not into reading technical books or playing mind-training games." The good news is that learning doesn't have to be boring, and it doesn't need to look like it did when you were in school. You don't have to read long books or listen to someone lecturing you. There are abundant ways to stimulate your brain without feeling like you are going to die of boredom, or dredging up old painful memories of feeling dumb in chemistry class. Reading a book, magazine, or blog for pleasure; listening to an informational podcast or an audiobook; playing cards; solving crosswords; playing Wordscapes or other games on your smartphone; visiting a museum; or engaging in healthy debate on a topic you're passionate about—all these fun activities also exercise your brain.

What Do You Want Your Brain to Do for You?

To take care of our brains, we need a clear understanding of all that our brains do for us. The following is a list of activities your brain makes possible for you:

- Competing
- Contemplating
- Cooperating
- Creating
- Deciding
- Expressing emotions
- Focusing
- Judging
- Labeling (experiences and emotions)
- Meditating
- Moving (walking, running, playing, etc.)
- Observing
- Perceiving
- Planning
- Praying
- Processing new information
- Reading
- Remembering
- Responding to my environment
- Speaking/communicating
- Studying
- Thinking
- Understanding
- Using my intuition

In your notebook, jot down the top three brain activities that are most important to you. For each item, respond to these three questions:

1. "What does this brain function allow me to do that matters to me?"

Here are two examples:
Creating helps me come up with new ways of organizing my home.
Perception helps me to be able to smell.

2. "Why is that important to me?"

Here are two examples:
Creating new ways of organizing my home is important because it helps me maintain structure and feel in control of my life.
I need to be able to smell because I enjoy scented candles.

3. "What am I doing to nurture this brain function so that it stays strong?" If nothing, what can you start doing to nurture this brain function?

Here are two examples:

To help my brain to think to the best of its ability, I am willing to start listening to a podcast that emphasizes organization and productivity.

To help me to enhance my perception, I am willing to practice mindfulness to deepen my ability to savor the candle-scents I enjoy.

The list of what our brain does for us is virtually endless, and the same is true for the ways we can help support it so that it functions at its best. Start with a straightforward act today to help your brain to do what you need and want it to do.

Now try it yourself !

1. What does this brain function allow me to do that matters to me?

_____

_____

_____

_____

_____

2. Why is that important to me?"

_____

_____

_____

3. What am I doing to nurture this brain function so that it stays strong? If nothing, what can I start doing to nurture this brain function?

_____

_____

_____

_____

Engage

If you're like most people, it's probably been a while since you've thought about all the things your brain does for you, much less considered exercising your brain. This part shows you why prioritizing intellectual self-care is essential, and how to start doing it. Simply put, intelligent self-care keeps us sharp and growing. One of the easiest methods to ward off boredom or feel stuck is to keep challenging yourself to learn and grow.

Where to Start: Learn More About an Interesting Topic

We all find certain things interesting. Learning more about the topics you already enjoy can be a great place to start when you want to stimulate your brain. Grab your notebook and make a list of all the issues, activities, sports, places, people, and even animals you find interesting - things you're curious about, that excite you, and really hold your attention.

Make a list of topics you find interesting

_____   _____

_____   _____

_____   _____

_____   _____

Once you have this list, think about ways to learn more about the stuff that interests you. For instance, one of my favorite sports to watch is boxing. I admire the amount of technique and skill it takes to have the stamina to last 12 rounds in the ring, and I love the fact that, at any moment, one move can change the whole fight. The excitement of it all is thrilling to me! One way I've used my joy for boxing to contribute to my intellectual self-care is by getting to know specific boxers. I treat it like a fun history lesson, and search for articles about the man or woman behind the gloves. In the process of doing this research I'm gaining new knowledge, which helps me to feel more connected to the sport. After I learn something new about a particular boxer, I share the information with my husband. By recalling what I learned and sharing this information, I'm exercising my memory.

One of my colleagues enjoys keeping track of current events in the lives of her favorite celebrities. How about you? Can you think of a topic you'd enjoy reading about online or in a magazine?

Try Something New: Learn a Language

Learning a new language is a wonderful way to feed your brain and keep it in shape. It helps you to keep your mind sharp, by demanding that it must translate information that you read or heard in your native language, to the language you are learning. At the same time, learning a new language sharpens your communication skills and opens up the possibilities for you to create new relationships with people who speak the language you're learning.

There are numerous "cool" ways to learn a new language these days. There are books, apps, study abroad programs, and individual language coaches. And there are tons of languages to learn! Take a moment to consider what language you might be interested in learning. Take one step in that direction by downloading a language-learning app on your phone, and spending some time exploring the app.

Making the Time: Find "Free Moments" for Intellectual Stimulation

What if I told you that creating time for intellectual stimulation doesn't necessarily require you to carve out time in your schedule? It can be as modest as repurposing the time you already have. We all have "free moments" that sneak by each day without our even recognizing it. For example, moments tick by while we are waiting for appointments, classes, or meetings to begin; while commuting to and from work; while standing in line or sitting on hold; while commercials are playing; and so on. This doesn't even include the time we spend checking our phones and scrolling through social media.

Imagine if you decided to repurpose just a fraction of these "free moments" into intellectual self-care. Here are ideas for doing just that:

• Listen to an audiobook or podcast.
• Read a newspaper, book, or blog.
• Play a game on your smartphone that requires you to think, solve a problem, or be creative.
• Engage with a language learning app.
• Nurture your creativity by coming up with an invention that would make your life easier.
Taking just a few moments for these mind-stimulating activities when you would otherwise be wasting time waiting for something to happen goes a long way in nurturing your intellectual self-care.

Discover

Sometimes it can be hard to know (or remember!) what truly interests us. Life has a way of pulling us toward doing the things that are necessary, like paying bills and keeping our household running (in other words, adulting) to the extent that we can forget we also need to be engaging our mind in meaningful ways. If we give ourselves the chance to wake up out of the fog of being on autopilot, we might realize that we don't even know what topics or hobbies we find intriguing. This "Get to Know Your Interests" activity can lay the foundation for discovering what appeals to you most and which interests and pastimes are going to feed your brain the nourishment it needs.

Get to Know Your Interests

One way to learn more about topics that excite you is to pay close attention to how you feel when you're engaging in different activities to try to stimulate your mind. To get you started, here's a list of topics to choose from, or come up with your own:

- Climate
- Culture
- Geography
- History
- Law
- Mathematics
- Medicine
- Mental health
- Movies
- Music
- Politics
- Public health
- Science
- Technology
- Visual/performing arts
- Women's issues/history

Now, create a grid like the one that follows. I've included an example for you to follow. For the next week, commit yourself to "trying out" a topic or activity to see how much it interests and excites you on a scale of 0 to 10, where 0 is not at all interested or excited and 10 is extremely interested or excited.

To explore the new topic, come up with an activity that exposes you to it. Possible actions include reading about the case, listening to a podcast on the subject, talking to someone whose work revolves around that topic, or researching the topic on the Internet. Pay attention to how you feel when you are engaging in the activity. Notice whether you get absorbed in it and are eager to learn more or if you quickly lose interest. Pay attention to the types of thoughts and feelings you have while you are "trying out" the topic. The more excited and interested you feel, the more likely this is a topic you enjoy and may want to explore on a deeper level to nourish your mind.

Getting to Know Myself Log

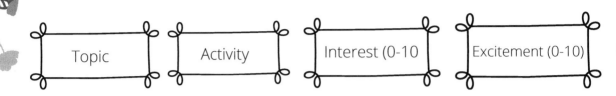

Topic	Activity	Interest (0-10)	Excitement (0-10)
Example: History	Visit a Local Museum	6	8

Be Excited

Maybe it's been years since you've taken the time to think about the topics and ideas that really excite you. Make today the day you give yourself consent to reconnect with your intellectual side and really discover what topics make you feel eager to learn more. The following activity can help you to remember what ideas and intellectual pursuits are exciting to you.

Reward Yourself

To reward yourself for nurturing your intellectual self-care, take a trip to your local bookstore or browse the book tab of your favorite online retailer. Give yourself ample time to browse around and check out different genres. Buy any book that strikes your fancy. It doesn't have to be serious or intellectual - just anything that involves your mind. It could be a book of jokes or a paperback romance. Don't forget to actually take the time to read your new book for pleasure and to stimulate your mind.

Learn

Now that you have a better idea of the types of topics that excite you, it's time to start learning more about them. There are a variety of ways to learn—it's not all reading books and taking notes! You can acquire new knowledge by listening to experts on the radio or podcasts, doing something new with your hands, watching YouTube videos, and doing exercises that test the new knowledge you're gaining along the way.

Keep in mind that to really master a new skill or topic, you should practice it and engage with it consistently. Aim for daily or weekly contact to ensure the new knowledge really sinks in. For instance, if you want to learn the skill of driving, it is best to practice a few times a week to begin to master the skill. If you drive one day for one hour and don't drive again for several weeks, that increases the chances you will lose the new skills you acquired during your first lesson. Since you've picked topics that you find interesting or are otherwise motivated to pursue, working them into your weekly schedule should be fun.

What new skill(s) can you learn ?

_____

_____

_____

CHAPTER 14

SELF-LOVE

3 Self-Love Activities to Make You Love Yourself More

#1 — Write Self-Love Quotes, Affirmations, and Inspirations - "I am the apple of my eye, the light of motivation I pursue" — Ntathu. "Every day I love myself more and more" — Ntathu. "The more I respect and appreciate myself, the more I develop within" — Ntathu. Build your affirmations or choose the 3 above, and write them down. You can sneak your affirmations into your handbag as an extra treat to yourself, or write them out on your phone and read them to yourself during the day, especially when you feel anxious. You will immediately relax into the more caring side of your being.

#2 Pray and Show Gratitude for Your Health and Wellness - If you're not religious, you may be confused by the thought of meditation. I understand that, as I went through a phase of challenging "Jesus and all that sacred stuff" after my brother and cousin passed away, but that brought me to a more meaningful and soulful link with life over the years. Over the years, though, I now appreciate the importance of spending a few minutes in quiet contemplation and prayer. If you practice a religious belief, find some prayers and guidelines for prayer that give you peace, joy and meaning on the inside.

If you're not sure what to use and you're waiting quietly, I've composed a prayer of thanks that I'm happy to share with you. Take a moment and utter the prayer below: "Dear God (or Divinity if you prefer), thank you for the grace that runs from my heart openly, for the love and devotion that I now offer to myself; for the emergence of boundless energy and rivers of goodwill. Thank you, Mother Earth, for the endless streams of life that float into my mind now, endlessly enriching my life and filling me up until I overflow; for the sense of peace and a peaceful heart. I am purely awesome and I hope forevermore to be part of the streams flowing in creation, blessing others and being blessed myself. Thank you, Holy God, for granting me the reason to value myself."

#3 Meditate. If you're doing meditation, you'll know it's one of the best gifts. There are plenty of meditations out there, and you will come across different techniques and insights during your self-love path.

As a novice, studying and acquiring yoga, for example, from an experienced teacher is always better.

Here's a guided Self-Love Meditation for you to practice. After you've spoken your three everyday affirmations, finished your morning teacup, then your every-day Gratitude Prayer, find a quiet space, put your phone on a 3-minute timer to make yourself comfortable, take a few steady breaths in and out of your nose, lower your shoulders and read the following passage to yourself loudly. Sit in silence after you have read it, and take a couple more minutes remaining still before re-engaging with your day as the timer stops.

Guided Self-Love Meditation

I breathe in calm; I breathe out love. I breathe in warmth; I breathe out pleasure. I breathe in forgiveness; I let go of the pain and sorrow. I breathe in love and happiness, I let go of the misery. I breathe in life and groove in sync with the rhythms of my core.

Closing Thoughts and Call to Action

I urge you to set aside 15 minutes to follow these clear habits of self-care as you wake up for the next 5 days. When you begin your day, you will feel refreshed, energized, and the best of all, cherished and nurtured. I would love to know how you're getting on.

Finding Your Way to Self-Love

It's the mystery we're both posing as we recover and rebuild broken self-esteem. We want to respect ourselves more thoroughly, and enjoy ourselves. We certainly know the anguish of creeping into those old feelings of worthlessness. They learn how we are most "sensitive" and self-critical.

But how do we get to feel self-love from these wincing, self-denying feelings on earth? How do we value ourselves when we don't respect ourselves so clearly in many ways?

Do not be depressed if you feel this annoyance. It will often seem like "you really can't get there from here" in finding your way to self-love. This obvious impasse is to be anticipated.

And this is why: we must first feel full and nourished to feel happy and feel a positive sense of self. Of course, the issue is that these self-negative feelings discourage us from being satisfied and filled properly.

This is especially true as our sense of self, our self-image, our entire personality falls heavily into these hurt emotions. Since we "tell" ourselves mainly through this injury — that we are not enough (not adequately great, not sufficiently small, not sufficiently achieved, not sufficiently "complete," etc.) — we rob ourselves of that essential, continuous nourishment that we need to encounter more.

So, our double-binding is here. We can't see our worthiness to be filled; and to see our worthiness, we can't fill ourselves. So how are we supposed to get there?

Thankfully, the Bridge to Self-Love is an intermediate step, a "condition" that bridges the gap between that state of self-rejection and deficiency and the normal sense of self-love. It's a place that allows us to keep getting nourished, even given the self-negative feelings, so we can restore and reawaken the inherent sense of being all right and necessary.

And the middle position is self-acceptance and respect for oneself. Unlike that mystical, distant land of self-love, it's remarkably easy to find this intermediate place... And incredibly strong.

Self-acceptance and kindness are not about trying to convince yourself that you are good or effective (or whatever) at the moment when your damaged emotions warn you that you are not. And it's not about having to kill yourself and correct what's "wrong" with you so you can fulfill the intense, perfectionist vision. Neither of these responses gives you a lot.

Getting into this middle position requires nothing more than handling oneself, in reaction to these painful feelings and stressful times, with patience and compassion.

Let's be clear about this. These wounded feelings you don't deny. And you don't doubt it's hard. You simply respond to these painful feelings in a different way.

Serving 'You' Instead of the Wounded Feelings

You're taking a different 'role.' You're taking a step backward and realizing that, as intense as these wounded feelings sound, they're just that: wounded feelings. They are feelings that a wounded place creates. They don't give you precise information about your dignity. They only warn you of a hurt, wounded position. And you choose to be compassionate, caring, and then healing toward yourself in the first place, in reaction to that hurt position. Note the difference again. You choose to handle yourself with dignity, care, and compassion rather than crumble into these fake, self-negative feelings. Instead of believing them, viewing yourself as a corrupt person, and driving yourself even harder... By adding kindness and understanding to this painful place, you react to this painful signal. Note, it is not about "fixing" yourself to regain your self-esteem. It's about self-FEEDING. Your task is not to please yourself or your life's "wounded" perception. Your task is to fix the wound that is at the heart of it: to feed the poor, judging spot.

And you do this by coming to this position with patience and compassion rather than harshness.

In reality, a sign of your bruised self-esteem is that seemingly-good determination and toughness to repair yourself. Can you see that a strict response is actually a continuation of the biting, refusing behavior?

So, if you choose to treat yourself calmly and compassionately instead, you break that self-hardened pattern. Despite terms of what you "know" is wrong with you, when you can step back to continue to be compassionate and embrace yourself, the real sense within you continues to be nourished.

It's waking up. Your positive sense of self becomes stronger and stronger when you pursue this strategy.

And just to be sure about that, self-acceptance doesn't discourage you from taking positive steps for your growth and progress... or making the necessary changes in your life. These efforts require you to be particularly supportive, patient, and self-approving. This is the very strength you need to recover, improve, and push on.

An RX for those excruciating moments of self-rejection. Needless to say, kindness and empathy probably won't be your main reaction when that sense of worthlessness first raises its ugly head. We're going to want to crumble into these painful emotions at first. So, when this happens, we just need to pull back a bit and remember that these feelings are not accurate. These are injured feelings that take you to a wounded place. Let the discomfort remind you to be gentle and healing with yourself.

For these difficult moments, give it what I call a "drug". And the more these positions become sensitive and unpleasant, the more caring, gentle, and cautious you need to be with yourself. Also, the challenge we encounter in learning to love ourselves is that the particularly painful emotions correlated with damaged self-esteem have the unpleasant capacity to "erase" our sense of self-esteem and self-worth altogether. In essence, we can't find love for ourselves.

We have to be prepared for this very "natural" answer to our wound. And consider it with sympathy.

Patience and sympathy, thankfully, are expressions of kindness. Especially when they are directed at you. And this little move will start to bring you back to yourself immediately: back to fullness and back to life.

3 Symptoms That Show You Your Self-Love Deficiency

It may seem like a senseless question at first, "Will you esteem yourself?" but it's a very significant question that deserves a true answer. Does it make you smile when you hear this question, or does it make you cringe a little? This would be your first sign of the above issue, based on your response. If you respect yourself, when you are confronted with this problem you should be able to feel good. Check out the 3 indicators below that will alert you whether you lack self-love, or if you are all right here. First, ask yourself if you believe that self-love is an act of selfishness. Most people believe it's a false love, or it's selfish. They think it's not real. Have you ever heard of the saying, "If you don't respect yourself, nobody else can love you?" That assertion has so much validity, because knowing oneself provides an awareness of how to live. Secondly, do you need other people around you to praise you? If you are constantly searching for approval, this is also a good indicator of lacking self-love. It's a must to know how to create internal self-love. Thirdly, do you need to make others happy about your own feeling happy? If you're trying to make someone happier for the sake of yourself, and only having a little joy, then it's time to ask yourself, why? It's okay to enjoy doing things that make others happy, but if it's not in balance with your happiness, it might be another sign that you're lacking self-love. Don't hesitate if you lack self-love. It's easy to create. The first move is to realize that you need it.

EXERCISES

What are some positive affirmations you can say to yourself to practice self-love?

_____

_____

_____

_____

Write a small prayer for you to say

_____

_____

_____

_____

_____

_____

What kind of meditations can you do for yourself every day?

_____

_____

_____

_____

_____

Write down all your qualities and accept yourself for each and every one of them

_____

_____

_____

_____

_____

Do you often do things to make others happy even though you are not happy? If so, what do you usually do and how can you prioritize yourself from now on?

_____

_____

_____

_____

_____

_____

I feel so good when ...

_____

_____

_____

_____

_____

Imagine you have a Free Day to yourself: no "shoulds", no plans. What would be really satisfying to do?

_____

_____

_____

_____

_____

I wish I had more time for...

_____

_____

_____

_____

_____

I forgive myself for...

_____

_____

_____

_____

_____

_____

I will no longer blame myself for...

_____

_____

_____

_____

_____

_____

I give myself permission to let go of...

_____

_____

_____

_____

_____

_____

My biggest effort with self-love is...

_____

_____

_____

_____

_____

_____

I promise myself to never...

_____

_____

_____

_____

_____

_____

What does self-love mean to you?

_____

_____

_____

_____

_____

What is holding you back?

_____

_____

_____

_____

_____

_____

Write a letter to your teenage-self

_____

_____

_____

_____

_____

_____

Write a letter to your future self

CHAPTER 15

WOMEN AND ROMANTIC RELATIONSHIPS

In this chapter I want to talk especially to younger women, but I am going to make points anyone can benefit from. I feel like I've given you some good tools to have before you throw yourself into a romantic relationship, if that is something you even want at this point in your life. We've worked on building self-esteem - you're working towards building self-confidence; and now I feel we can talk about dating.

Are You Ready?

There's a lot to talk about here. The first thing is you must be sure that you are ready. Why? Because as I mentioned earlier, dating comes with lots of compromises, and most times, disappointments. Dating is not as laid-back as it seems, and it really shouldn't be. Dating shouldn't be a time of having sex, moving in with each other, and doing everything that a marriage entails. Dating should be a time of getting to know each other as platonic friends, which will allow you the clarity to decide if this person is right for you; and if you can be happy with this person long-term. If your dating experiences are all easy right now: no arguments, no disagreements, etc. then one of you is, or both of you are not being true to yourselves. And considering you are learning self-love and still trying to figure out what your real needs are, to begin with, this is probably true. You have probably been saying "yes" to everything you won't be saying "yes" to in 10 years, because you are going to be a more mature person with, hopefully, clearly defined boundaries.

There are so many things to consider before you decide to date somebody. Many of us wish we had this information before we started dating, as clearly as you are about to get it here. When I was a kid, I was simply instructed not to date. Not that I listened anyway: that was too clear-cut; I couldn't understand why I couldn't date. I don't want that to be a problem for you. So, I am going to try to help you to understand all the things I believe you should know when you are ready to date, or if you've been in relationships before, when you are ready to start again.

So, are you ready? Why do you or why don't you think so?

_____

_____

_____

_____

Slow Down

The second thing is to avoid being in a hurry to have sex with him. I can't stress this enough. Every single man I've talked to who did not just want a woman to have sex with (they do exist), have confirmed to me that if he loves a woman, he is eager to wait until she is ready for sex. Now that you know this, get to know him well. It's called "dating" for a reason. You are supposed to go out and do things together so that you get to learn about the person; their likes, dislikes, what makes them angry, happy, sad, etc. You are supposed to inquire about their family; what's their family like? This is a huge one. Do they come from a broken home, or are their parents still married? If their parents are divorced, how has this affected them? How do the divorced parents get along? What are holidays like with their family? Do they trust others? Do they believe that people can be in love with persons other than themselves? There are so many things to learn in the dating process if it's done correctly, rather than the way some of us did it.

For those of you who are younger, let me illustrate this with a story. There is a young lady who took the time to date while she was in high school. She was not sexually intimate with the young man. They went to movies together, summer camps, basketball games, retreats, and did all sorts of fun things together. They dated for about two years. She reports that she is glad she waited to give her body to him, and didn't rush, because she found out during the dating period that he is not a man that can commit himself to one woman. While they were dating, and getting to know each other, he was asking her other friends out, and she even found him kissing one of her friends! She explained to me that if she had already given her body to him, it would have been harder for her to leave him because she would have doubted whether any other "good guy" would have wanted to be with her. She said because she was not sexually active with him, it was easy for her to leave him and just focus on herself. She also explained that she was hurt and felt betrayed, but she was able to overcome the hurt and betrayal because she knew that she was true to herself, and felt very good about protecting herself the way she did. She concluded, "I don't feel like I sold myself short. I loved myself enough to hold on and find out who he was."

What is your typical pattern of being intimate with a man?

_____

_____

_____

_____

How soon or late does it happen?

_____

_____

_____

_____

Is this something you'd like to change? If so, how will you change it?

_____

_____

_____

_____

Goals, Goals, Goals

The third thing you should do is make sure you talk to him about your goals and ask him about his. This is not something that is beyond what you can and should do. Don't think little. Think big, and ahead. Think like the confident, self-assured woman that you are. This is how you will know if the two of you are on the same path, to begin with. What if he doesn't want to go to college and you want to? Maybe you are both in the twelfth grade and he plans to finish high school and go work in his father's meat shop? Is that something you are okay with? If you are, then great! It works. But what if you are not, and you never asked him? What do you think is going to happen when you are preparing to leave for college, and he is staying to work with his dad? Anything could happen. It could be a recipe for a breakup, or it could work because that is what you want. If it is not what you want, though, and you break up, then you will have wasted time that could have been spent dating someone else who had similar interests. By the way, this is what dating several people means. It doesn't mean you sleep with one and break up, then another one, and another one. It means, in the words of my father, "you socialize" with that person as you figure out if they are a match for you or not.

You know what's sad: the people who become perfect at doing this are women who were once married, got divorced and have learned that there is truly nothing to rush. If you are a mature woman, you'll understand this, whatever your experiences have been. It would be pleasant to have more young women doing this so that they can enjoy their relationships better with people they are compatible with. I believe if young women took the time to do this, the divorce rate would be lower. You wouldn't be getting married because you had butterflies in your stomach. You would be getting married because the butterflies came and left, and you could still enjoy this person's company. That is love!

It's friendship that keeps romantic relationships, especially marriage, going for a lifetime. When you marry someone that you are friends with, you have a healthier marriage. You can share anything with them and know that they wouldn't judge you. You can both laugh about silly things. You can be honest with each other even when it's uncomfortable. You are their biggest champion, yet are honest with them, when you must be - you do not lie to them. Your marriage is not about proving to others that you have a good relationship; it's about proving to yourselves that you are determined to make your relationship healthy and long-lasting. You wouldn't be doing anything in public that you don't practice in private, because your marriage is not for show: it's real. Consequently, you want to take your time and build a friendship; a real solid relationship before rushing to the altar or getting in bed with the guy. To be honest, I don't think you need to be worrying about marriage at this stage, anyway. I am hoping that what this book does for you, is help you see all your potential and help you plan your life so that you are in a secured, matured place before you even consider marrying someone.

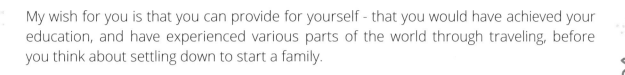

My wish for you is that you can provide for yourself - that you would have achieved your education, and have experienced various parts of the world through traveling, before you think about settling down to start a family.

What are some of your goals that you would want your partner/future partner to understand?

_____

_____

_____

_____

_____

Set Clear Boundaries

The fourth thing is to set clear boundaries. What things will you not tolerate? My mother told me never to let a man hit me, even if he pretended to be joking. Warn him after the first "joke" and walk away at the attempt of the second. I'm going to tell you that I took this advice very seriously, and for me, it even mattered how he spoke to me and what tone of voice he spoke to me in. It was just that important for me. You know the things that matter to you, and those things that are offensive to you or make you doubt yourself. Be very clear about them very early in your dating life. Are you okay with your boyfriend being friends with his ex-girlfriend? If not, then do not encourage it, because you don't want to lose him. If he respects and values you, once you explain to him why you are uncomfortable with that kind of relationship, he will cut it off. Do not settle for poor treatment in hopes that he will learn, or fear that you will lose him if you start making demands early. Reasonable demands can and should be made early in a relationship. Unreasonable demands should never be made. Never ask a man to put you before his mother: that is unreasonable. He came into this world, first because of God, and then his mother. Should you decide tomorrow that you do not want a relationship with him any more, it is his mother that will be there to support him, however he might need her to. You have the right to ask a man to put you before his friends; that is reasonable. His friends cannot take your place, those are two different types of relationships.

When his friends leave, it is you that he will have in his corner. By the way, his friends should be focusing on their own relationships, not taking up all his time.

Basically, you are the one who determines what those boundaries are, so make sure you know what you will bear in a relationship and what you are not willing to. What you love, you don't hurt. You don't take a knife and chop off your hands if you are mentally well, because you love your hands and need them to do various things in life. If the boy loves you, he wouldn't do things to hurt you or lower your self-esteem and self-confidence. If he's doing those things, he's not worth your time.

What are your boundaries? List them below

_____

_____

_____

_____

_____

_____

_____

_____

_____

_____

Know Your Worth

The fifth thing is to know your worth. I mean this. I don't care if you come from a divorced household, or you were raised by a single mother or father, or you were a "troubled kid" who went to the principal's office every day and got detention regularly. You are worthy of respect, unconditional love, and care, and anybody who wants to be in a relationship with you must understand that. They must rise to meet you. None of the circumstances I described above give anyone permission to treat you poorly. People divorce for various reasons and none of those should be blamed on a child. If you were young and made mistakes, no one has the right to use that against you for the rest of your life. If that boy wants you romantically, then he must accept you as you are, or he can keep walking. There is somebody who will love you for you. Do not allow anyone to use your family history or your past against you, especially when you've forgiven yourself. You deserve better than that.

Write down the affirmation "I am worthy and deserve love, respect and care" as many times as you can

_____

_____

_____

_____

_____

_____

_____

CHAPTER 16

LEARN HOW TO SAY "YES" AND WHEN TO SAY "NO"

Say "Yes" to Life

We all have these things that we keep putting off for 'Someday.' Someday we'd wear our favorite dress, join the ballet class, learn piano, take out that fine china for dinner, and what not. Yet the only time we have is this present moment.

A lot of people reach the end of their earthly life feeling as if they never got a chance to be truly alive. There is nothing worse than regret. Tomorrow you will regret everything you didn't do today. Also, when you constantly put off living until tomorrow, you never end up fully appreciating all the gifts that you have today.

In order to completely embrace life and make the most of it in the here and now, you must show up at your best. Wear your best clothes, use your fine china for meals, do what you really want to do on a daily basis; as if today were the last day of your life (because one day you are going to be right about it...). When death comes, most people don't regret the mistakes they made as much as they regret the time that they lost which they could have spent in being truly alive.

I want you to say "YES" to those things that you've been putting off for later. No one knows how long they are going to live, so why not make the most of the here and now by doing exactly what you want to do.

I would also highly recommend that you start wearing your best clothes on a daily basis. Make an effort to look good. Put your best foot and face forward, even if no one other than you yourself is going to be looking at you.

There is something tremendously empowering in making an effort to look our best. It automatically helps us to feel better about ourselves and more confident. I don't mean that you have to wear your silk gown every day – just clothes you enjoy wearing and feel confident in.

Generally, how we choose to dress has a strong effect on how we choose to conduct ourselves. For instance, it is much easier to slump in your PJs than it is to do in a pencil skirt. Raise the bar for yourself – look your best, be your best, behave at your best every day because who knows, this might be the only day you have for doing everything you want to do!

Don't save your china for guests – use them for your daily meals because you are special, and you deserve to be treated that way. Don't have 'home' clothes and 'going out' clothes. Wear your best clothes every day. In the evening, retire into your night wear for sleeping – not just old worn-out clothes but actual night wear. When you treat yourself as the most special person in your world, the whole Universe conspires to prove that you are right in believing so.

Tasks:

• Make a list of all the things that you have been putting off doing – things that really matter to you, and doing them will make you feel good. Make sure that you do at least one of them.

• Wear the clothes that you truly like. Do this even if no one else other than you will be seeing you. In the end, the only person whose opinion of you truly matters is your own. Don't forget that when you start loving and admiring yourself, others start doing the same, because our relationships with others are only a reflection of our relationship with our own self. Wearing the clothes that you really like and feel confident in is a way of saying that you matter. You deserve to look your best, not for anyone else, but for your own self.

• Use your favorite crockery for meals even if you'd be eating all your meals alone. By living life exactly the way you want to, you send a powerful message to the Universe that you are grateful for all the blessings that have come to you so far. At the same time, you are ready for many more amazing experiences to come your way.

Try it now. What are some things you have been putting off doing? List them below:

_____

_____

_____

_____

_____

_____

_____

Learning to Say NO

Just as saying "Yes" to life is important, saying "NO" at the right time and place is equally important. A lot of times we say "yes" to the wrong things for the wrong reasons. Usually, this happens when we don't want to disappoint the other person. We make a compromise with our own wishes and agree to something that doesn't feel good to our heart.

The problem with this is that even though you end up looking good to the other person, you are letting your own self down. You are bound to feel resentful and also angry (most likely) towards yourself and towards that person.

It's very important to know who you are as a person, what your values are, what you are okay with, and what you are not okay with. This will help you to set powerful boundaries. Not having boundaries will constantly make you feel as if you are being pushed in different directions by other people. Taking a firm stand for yourself is necessary for living a happy and fulfilling life.

I want to ask you to get in touch with your heart more deeply than ever. Every time someone asks you for something, don't just jump to answer it. Take a few moments and gauge how you feel inside your heart. Say "yes", only if you truly want to say so. Saying "NO" gently but firmly is an art. It is surely one of the most important skills one can have!

We usually take life for granted. We think we have forever to live, so we spend a lot of time doing those things that we don't really want to do but feel obliged to do. I am challenging you to understand and fully appreciate the fact that every day of life is a gift – one that can be taken away from you at any moment, any day.

What if this is your last day, would you still say Yes" to whatever it is you are considering doing at this moment? If the answer is "NO" then just say "No" and walk away. You might not be able to make everyone happy, but that's all right. It's not your responsibility to make everyone happy. The only person whose happiness is solely and completely your responsibility is you yourself.

People are bound to get upset when you don't give them what they want from you but that's all right too. You have to be relaxed with the chance that sometimes in the process of ensuring your own happiness and doing what's best for you, you will unwittingly upset other people. How they deal with it is up to them.

You are not obliged to do their bidding. This is not selfish or egoistic. Sometimes saying "no" is the most loving thing to do, as by doing that you are honoring your soul while offering your Truth to the other person. As a rule of thumb, never say "yes" to someone if that will leave you burning with rage and resentment inside.

Now, there might be some situations where saying "no" is just not possible or at least the consequences of saying "no" will be so severe that you won't be able to handle the repercussions.

I would say that there is a way around everything. You can at least express to the other person that you don't really want to say "yes" but are feeling obliged to do so. This might help you both in reaching a compromise.

If even this does not seem do-able, and you feel like there is no way out, then I would suggest trying to see what you can learn from this experience. Try to see it as something that is going to help you to become a better person. It might seem impossible to glean such wisdom from it at the moment, but try to find the pearl hidden in the oyster.

At the end of the day, just recall that it is not worth doing anything with resentment and anger in your heart. Therefore, I will still say that sticking with your own Truth is always the best choice. Say "NO" to anything that your heart doesn't agree with.

Eventually, you have to become comfortable with people not liking it when you say "no", especially when you distinguish in your heart that you are doing the right thing. You can't please everyone, and that's all right. Everyone is responsible for their own happiness. Your responsibility is your own happiness, first and foremost.

Besides, you are causing more damage to your relationship with that person by saying a "yes" that is fraught with tension and resentment. A loving and firm "NO" is much better than a resentful "Yyes" in the long-run. The more firmly you establish your boundaries, the more people will be willing to respect it. It might not occur right away, but eventually this will surely be the case.

For now, I'd urge you to say "NO" to all those activities, food, places and people that don't serve your highest good. For instance, if getting in shape has been on your list, then saying "NO" to junk food and "yes" to the gym should be on your agenda. Don't put off things for an elusive tomorrow.

Our time on this earth is finite and limited at best. Learn to act in the here and now! You want to gain every experience that your heart craves, and end every day with the satisfaction that you lived the day as best as you could while making the most of every opportunity that came your way.

Therefore, say "NO" to procrastination. Say "NO" to all your bad habits. Make small changes today and act on them, because the journey of a thousand miles always starts with a small step in the right direction.

If you feel confused, then listen more attentively to your intuition – your heart has all the answers that you are seeking. You just have to quieten the din of your mind to hear the voice of your soul. Let all your actions, words and thoughts be guided by your higher self. Put your heart and soul in every moment – live every day as if it were your last. You'll be amazed by the miracles you manage to create!

Task:

Say "NO" to all the things, people and circumstances that don't resonate with your soul. It might not be easy to implement this fully, but at least make a start somewhere. Say NO to at least one thing that doesn't feel right to you. Free yourself from anger and resentment. Every time you do something because you HAVE to do it, rather than because you truly want to do it, you are building resentment. Nothing is more destructive than the emotions of anger and resentment. Stay away from them as much as conceivable.

Are there some things you want to say "NO" to, but are unable to? What are they?

_____

_____

_____

_____

_____

_____

_____

_____

_____

How do you feel when someone does not respect your decision to say "NO"?

_____

_____

_____

_____

_____

How can you encourage yourself be strong enough to say "NO" when you need to?

_____

_____

_____

_____

_____

_____

CHAPTER 17

LET GO

Did you grow up with a blueprint in your mind of what you "should" become, based on what others have expected of you? Even if someone has wanted certain things for you with the best of intentions, their life-path may differ from yours. Others may have learned important lessons on their path and not want you to have to endure the same mistakes. You can graciously accept this wisdom and still be true to yourself.

To begin, think about what expectations you have internalized, via your environment, family, or society. What ideas of "success" have you absorbed or taken on from others?

Success can be defined differently for each life-path. Our paths are as unique as we are, as individuals, and feelings of accomplishment will be related to what our souls have set out to achieve. Maybe for some it is more career-based, and for others more relationship-focused. Maybe you love caring for children, or maybe your goal is to help animals be treated with more compassion. Maybe you even had different motivations in previous lifetimes—some people feel that our soul's intentions for this lifetime are what we hope to balance out from a past life.

You can do this without fear as long as you maintain your earthly values and responsibilities. This is your life, and it is a gift to all when you live it as your true self.

When you work with the universe, it is essential to establish a healthy amount of trust in the process and to relinquish the right amount of control. To begin safely letting go, prepare yourself to receive something that might not be exactly what you expected, but may be just what you needed.

What are some expectations you hold for yourself? Are any of them unrealistic?

_____

_____

_____

_____

_____

_____

Give Yourself Permission

As you develop your relationship with yourself, remember that you can give the universe permission to assist you, and you can give yourself permission to receive what you need. Imagine a tree, strongly rooted into the earth. While its roots go deep into the ground to receive nutrients, the branches reach up, as if in surrender, to receive the sunlight. The tree integrates earthbound support and receptive openness.

As you ground into your strong personal foundation and connection to Mother Earth, you will come closer to the roots of your truth. As you let go and open yourself to the process, you will receive your light from the universe. Through this integrated process, you will grow and blossom into your full self.

What are your expectations of who you think you "should" be and what your life "should" look like? Take a minute to reflect on what may have influenced these expectations. Did they come from your deepest soul's desires, society's rules, or others who have had a profound impact on your life? Devote five minutes to writing in your journal about the expectations you feel within. Give yourself permission to question these things and explore their origin in order to honor your true nature.

You Don't Need Approval

You don't need anyone else's approval. As long as you honor yourself spiritually and act with integrity, you are worthy, approved, good, and acceptable. That's it! All you have to do is be true to your core self. A big piece of this is learning to let go of others' expectations and opinions of you.

You may have been in circumstances where you felt you needed external approval in order to be loved or recognized as an integral part of society. It is natural to feel this way. Our culture sends many messages about what success looks like, especially in terms of financial, material, educational, and professional gains. Plus, the approval of someone important to you can feel like a green light to keep doing what you are doing.

But by giving someone else the power to approve your actions, and thus control you, you give away your personal power. You, and only you, can define your journey and purpose. The next time you're choosing whether or not to act or pursue a goal, ask yourself where this choice is coming from. Are you being guided by you yourself, or an outside influence? Finding that answer grows easier with practice.

What other people think is only that: what they think. Your truth is not determined by someone else's judgment of you. Your truth is determined by your soul and your actions. While it can be helpful to check in with others you trust (like your support network), their thoughts don't define you. You get to choose who you are and how you live. Perhaps true fulfillment comes from the good that you do for yourself and others. Only trust the thoughts of those who can clearly see your truth with a pure heart.

Are there any people in your life whose approval you seek? List them below:

_____

_____

_____

_____

You Are Accountable to You

We are all accountable to ourselves. Our actions do affect each other, but we are only responsible for the actions we take. We are all on our own personal voyages within an interconnected society. Being accountable to yourself also means standing up for what is right when necessary. Some circumstances are harder than others, but it is what we do within the circumstances that defines us. When you discover what truly matters to you, that will become your guiding light in any situation. Whatever you are faced with, peace and happiness can be found in the satisfaction of addressing what is on your path with integrity.

Imagine If ...

For the following scenarios, imagine taking the action truest to your heart. First, name at least three emotions you feel when considering taking each action. With conscious awareness of the possible judgments by others, imagine what would happen if you followed through anyway. After you have fully imagined the scenario, describe the best possible outcome in your journal.

1. You choose to wear your hair, clothes, or other physical adornment exactly in the way that best fits your personal truth. This can include paying no attention to these things because they do not interest you, spending a great deal of time on this method of self-expression because it is very important to you, or anything in between. In this situation, what feels right, comfortable, and befitting of you?

2. What truth would you speak? Are you holding back a valuable truth that would set you free? Should you speak up in the name of justice? What would you say?

3. Take a safe, well-calculated risk. What would be a bold step for you toward something you might enjoy? Do you want to start a conversation with someone? Audition for dance or theater? Sing at karaoke night? Why haven't you taken this step in the past? How can you take it now?

Little by Little

All of these steps are fragments of a gradual process of stepping out as your true self. As you go along, continue to check in with yourself and assess where you might be getting stuck. If you start to feel overwhelmed or unsatisfied, ask yourself: What do you need in order to feel safe enough to let go of outside influences?

Let's practice feeling safe. How do you currently feel when you go outside and interact with the world? To begin this exercise, I would like you to imagine what helps you feel safe when you go out as your true self. As you visualize going outside your door, describe how you see yourself from the perspective of someone who adores you. What anticipation do you feel before you set off to your destination? As you step out toward somewhere that inspires you, imagine the place you are going. What are you going to do when you get there? Describe your dream outing experience, who is there, and how you feel when you arrive. Imagine feeling safe as your true self during this experience. What good things happen? Write down the supportive factors that helped you feel secure in yourself during this imagery. Can you implement any of them today? Also include any necessary real-world precautions to keep yourself safe as you explore new territory.

Forgive Yourself

You may perceive some of your qualities as imperfect. Let's take a moment to celebrate that - it might be an indication of how your soul would like to grow in this lifetime. If anyone were perfect, they would have achieved full spiritual enlightenment and would probably not be here as a human on the earth plane. So, to honor the gift of your human experience, what would you like to learn and how would you like to grow? Do your perceived flaws interfere with your goals and values? If these "flaws" cause yourself or others harm, you can organize this to be your top priority to begin working on immediately. If it is only your perception that you are flawed in some way and this is causing you distress, check in to determine if your perception is accurate or if you are judging yourself based on external pressures. If you are being too tough on yourself, declutter your truth and embrace your strengths. This contributes to your well-being as well as to a more harmonious, heart-centered, and peaceful world.

If you know you need to work on some area, make it your next priority (after ensuring that you are doing no harm to self or others) to build your strength, learn, or grow in that area.

We are all working on ourselves throughout our lives, so just embrace that this is a healthy part of the process. Welcome your shadows into the light and build up the areas where you would like to direct your focus. Allow your spiritual self to guide your decisions and actions. You always have the answers within. This is hard work, and it is great that you are brave enough to do it!

Is there anything you need to forgive yourself for? Write it down here and forgive yourself ✒

_____

_____

_____

_____

Let Go of Anyone Holding You Back

You are almost ready to fly! We are now going to clear the space to open your wings by tapping into your intuition. Grab a pen and your journal and give yourself permission to be honest with yourself. Now answer this question with an immediate response:
What or who is holding you back?
Go ahead and write. Don't think too hard. Take as long as you need, and then consider this: Are you held back by something within yourself, or do you feel held back by an individual? If you feel that someone else does not have your best interest at heart, it is time to shed some light on the shadows of this connection. I want you to select all the reasons this connection is still in your life, and write any additional reasons not mentioned here:

- Fear
- Emotional codependency

- Guilt
- Obligation

- Financial dependency
- Anxiety about being alone

Other ✒

_____   _____   _____

_____   _____   _____

_____   _____   _____

_____   _____   _____

Obligations and responsibilities are important to our personal integrity. But sometimes they go too far and take us from our joy. By illuminating the nature of your connections and bringing honest awareness into your consciousness (instead of leaving them as shadows hidden in your subconscious), you can recognize your true responsibilities. Consider: do you really have a responsibility to this person? Or could you make some space in the relationship in order to tend to your well-being?

If we take too much accountability for someone else, that inhibits their own soul growth. We do not need to learn other people's lessons for them. Part of being accountable for yourself is taking care of yourself. So, thinking about your response to the previous question, how are you balancing your responsibilities for self with your responsibility for others?

Are you living your life with a healthy sense of personal accountability, or have you taken on too much of another person's soul work? Have codependent traits found their way into your relationships? There are many books on how to recognize and heal codependency.

You can create and maintain boundaries by verbally holding your ground and setting the example for how you allow others to treat you. Internal boundaries can be strengthened with self-care and not letting others' words get to you.

Shake off your feathers, hold your ground, live in your truth, and prepare to lift your spirit.

How will you let go of anything that is holding you back from today onwards? Write down all the ways below:

_____

_____

_____

_____

_____

CHAPTER 18

KEEP GOING

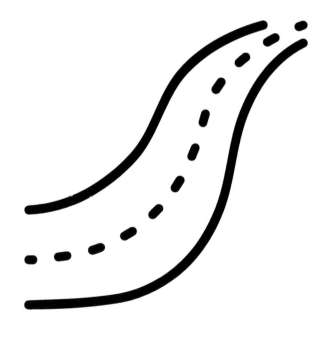

Getting to the top in any field takes grit, determination, and perseverance. These traits, along with passion and a willingness to work hard, create what's known as a winning mentality. Successful women recognize their talent, and they use it to realize their full potential. They set goals and pursue their own visions of success, but crucially, they persevere, always pushing themselves to be more of the person they aspire to be and do more of the things they feel most passionate about achieving.

The Vice-President of the USA

One such example of a successful woman is Kamala Devi Harris. She is the 49th Vice-President of the United States, and the first ever female incumbent of this office. She is also the highest-ranking female official in U.S. history, and the first African American and first Asian American vice president.

Kamala Harris was born in Oakland, California to a Jamaican father and an Indian mother, both academics. Her unusual background and family links have never set her back, and she went to primary school in a mostly-white area. Her parents divorced when she was seven, and again unusually for an American politician, she went with her mother to Canada where they lived in French-speaking Quebec. They practised kindness and generosity, we are told by her friend, when that friend was being abused by a stepfather, and took her in to live with them. This and her biologist mother's example inspired her to seek justice. She has visited and continued to keep contact with her parents' families outside the US, thus giving her an understanding of other cultures.

Kamala Harris studied politics and economics at Howard University in Washington D.C., and thereafter returned to California to attend law school at the University of California, where she was active in student affairs, and after studies was admitted to the California Bar in June 1990. From her work as a deputy district attorney, her career has been meteoric, and the sheer scope of her legal work is notable.

Harris has dealt with high rates of murders and homicides, more efficient and fairer convictions, the problem of repeat-offenders, and of school truancy. She has tackled powerful and corrupt individuals, helped to pass legislation to protect people who do not identify with traditional gender, and people who are attracted to the same sex, against violence and hate speech. Under her leadership, human trafficking, drugs and gun legislation have all been dealt with in updated procedures.

She has passed environmental legislation, and in the wake of the 2010 United States foreclosure crisis, led many efforts to stop people being evicted from their homes. She has also tackled banks and multinationals engaged in unfair charges and corrupt behavior.

Now she's the Vice-President! That's quite a career, not so? It wasn't just by working hard in one specialization (I'm not knocking that...) and so having no expertise in other fields; she's been willing to apply herself to whatever came along. Let her example and that of other successful women inspire you. It took hard work, a love of knowledge and willingness to face down injustice. Whatever you do, whoever you are, these virtues will get you far.

Kamala Harris's capacity to push boundaries and achieve professional success at each new stage of her career is something she has in common with many more powerful women throughout history. They share an attitude of grit, determination, and perseverance, and they see no limit to their potential achievements. Successful women keep pushing and keep growing, never allowing setbacks or failures to stop them in their tracks. They learn from setbacks and they try again, making whatever changes are necessary to keep moving in the direction of their goals. They continue playing until they get it right.

"True Grit"

"Grit" is a trait that we often associate with dogged determination, but psychology professor Angela Duckworth believes that true grit is a combination of perseverance and passion. Based on her research, Duckworth has concluded that determination alone is not enough to help someone to achieve a goal, if the goal is not something they feel passionate about achieving. This is something many successful women have demonstrated.

Just think: Dona Sarkar failed her computer science course, but she recognized her passion, talent, and potential, and tried again; Oprah Winfrey was demoted from news co-anchor to "morning cut-ins" in her early TV career; J. K. Rowling's manuscript for 'Harry Potter and the Philosopher's Stone' was famously rejected by 12 publishers before being accepted by Bloomsbury; and Arianna Huffington, President and Editor-in-Chief of the Huffington Post Media Group and writer of 13 books, had her second book rejected 36 times.

These women persevered in pursuit of their goals, but it was their passion that allowed them to succeed - their grit. "When you have a goal you care about so much that it gives meaning to almost everything you do," Duckworth says, "grit is holding steadfast to that goal. Even when you fall down. Even when you screw up. Even when progress toward that goal is halting or slow."

Characteristics of Grit

All successful women share a passion for what they do, but research has identified five characteristics that are common across all people with grit.

• Courage. Successful people are not afraid of failure, and gritty people accept failure as part of the learning process.

• Conscientiousness. Gritty people are achievement-oriented, meaning they work tirelessly to complete a task or project and they work hard at doing a good job.

• Endurance. Gritty people set long-term goals and commit themselves to seeing them through. They are prepared to do whatever it takes for as long as it takes, and they remain focused on the long-term vision.

• Resilience. Gritty people demonstrate resilience through optimism, confidence, and creativity. In simple terms, they have an underlying belief that things will work out and have the capacity to move on and try again even when they don't.

• Seeking excellence, not perfection. Gritty people prioritize progress over perfection. They strive to grow, move forward, push boundaries, and be the best they can be. Excellence does not require perfection.

Powerful women demonstrate these characteristics in everything they do, but they are traits that can be learned, developed, and practiced by anyone. With grit, determination, and perseverance, you, too, can achieve any goal and any level of success you aspire to.

Try This

Angela Duckworth recommends taking the following four steps to help you identify the goals you feel most passionate about and develop the grit you need to achieve them.

1. Pursue passions and interests. Thinking about the things that interest you is only the beginning. Angela recommends getting out and trying things to get hands-on experience before deciding whether it's a goal you feel you can be committed to achieving. You need genuine passion to develop the grit it takes to see something through.

2. Get started. It takes dedicated practice to develop skills. Feeling passionate about doing something makes it much more likely that you'll keep doing it, but it's only by doing it that you can progress and improve.

3. Find motivation through purpose. True grit comes through finding meaning in what you do. Successful women are purpose-driven. Be clear on why you are working toward a goal and draw on that reasoning to motivate and give purpose to your actions.

4. Keep believing. Maintain a positive mental attitude. Develop a growth mind-set to help you deal with setbacks. Successful women believe things can always get better because they can always take the action necessary to make change happen.

These steps tie in with the belief of legendary basketball coach John Wooden. He observed that the greatest achievers in the world, not just in sports but in all aspects of life, all share two common habits: they give themselves credit where credit is due, and they relentlessly pursue improvement.

Recognize your talents and potential, work hard at developing them, celebrate your every success and achievement—and keep going. Be relentless in your pursuit of excellence, and never give up on the goals that feed your passion.

What are your talents? List them below

_____

_____

_____

_____

_____

_____

_____

Write down sentences that give you credit for your talents and motivation

CONCLUSION

Thank you for reading this book. I hope I've helped you to gain some knowledge. 'Confidence and Self-Love: A Workbook for Women' is a must-read for any woman of any age looking to improve her self-esteem and confidence.

This book has given you the tools to take control of your life and work towards your goals. For women to continue to develop themselves, they have to ask questions and take the time to learn. This book appeals to women of all ages to join in on the conversation and make their voices heard.

I hope that this book has helped to empower you to do your best in all areas of your life. Recall, it is up to you to make the changes you want. If you aren't happy with something, change it. The Internet has made it "laid-back" for women to develop themselves. Women today have more options than ever before when it comes to tools, resources, and opportunities.

Know that to be able to be fully yourself, as a woman, you'll have to take the necessary steps to attain it. You have an option: you can make it happen, or not. No matter which choice you make, there are always going to be individuals out there who will tell you what they think is right for your life; but the only person who knows your true potential and capabilities is yourself. With a lot of hard work and determination, anything is possible in your life.

Throughout this book, you've learned that there's no such thing as a "one size fits all" solution. Women need to be active and decide what they want to do with their lives. There is a wide range of opportunities that are available for women to develop themselves.

If you have followed the steps that I've given you in this book, I know you will succeed. Remember, don't be afraid to ask for help, and be willing to take on new challenges. Although we were all born with the ability to help ourselves, we also need the support of others to reach our full potential. If you have succeeded, then give yourself a pat on the back and take some time out for yourself. You deserve it!

What are your goals for your life?

What kind of woman do you want others to see you as?

What are your plans for today?

Some days you won't feel like working, or perhaps it'll look like there's too much work that needs to be done... but push forward all the same!

No matter what happens in your life, remember why it's important to help yourself and why it's important to look after your mental health and emotional well-being. At times your mental health may not seem that important; but trust me on this one, when I say that it is vital for YOU!

When all else fails, remember what truly matters most in life: family, friends and being healthy.

Don't forget about these things.

In the end, I hope that this book has provided you with both information and inspiration. You might still be on your journey in self-care, or you may have already found a routine that works for you.

Thank you for finishing this book. It was a real pleasure to help you to learn. I hope that you enjoyed our trip, and that you found this guide useful on your future path.

many
thanks

NOTES

NOTES

Printed in Great Britain
by Amazon